BASIC PUBLIC
SPEAKING

BASIC PUBLIC SPEAKING

Patricia Bradley Andrews

Indiana University, Bloomington

1817

HARPER & ROW, PUBLISHERS, New York
Cambridge, Philadelphia, San Francisco,
London, Mexico City, São Paulo, Singapore, Sydney

Sponsoring Editor: **Louise H. Waller**
Project Editor: **Mary G. Ward**
Cover Design: **Jack Ribik**
Photo Research: **Mira Schachne**
Production: **Willie Lane**
Compositor: **ComCom Division of Haddon Craftsmen, Inc.**
Printer and Binder: **R. R. Donnelley & Sons Company**

BASIC PUBLIC SPEAKING

Library of Congress Cataloging in Publication Data

Andrews, Patricia Bradley.
  Basic public speaking.

  Includes index.
  1. Public speaking.   I. Title.
PN4121.A676 1985   808.5'1   84-22386
ISBN 0-06-040925-8

84 85 86 87 9 8 7 6 5 4 3 2 1

For Jennifer

CONTENTS

PREFACE

Whenever you make a public speech, you do so for a reason. Maybe you want to convince your classmates to join a group, to give blood to the Red Cross, or to become more informed about the causes of stress. Whatever your purpose, public speeches are tools designed to achieve something. Within ethical guidelines, the good speaker is one who is able to achieve his or her objectives.

Many times in your life you will be called upon to make a speech in public. "Not if I can help it!" you may be thinking. Yet, if you are planning to pursue a career as a professional, the chances are very good that you cannot help making just such a speech. You will be asked to speak again and again. Sometimes your speeches will be informal, as, for example, when you are asked to address a business meeting and make a few comments about a conference you recently attended. Or you may have a small staff that from time to time you brief on how to accomplish some task. If you become a manager or an officer in some organization, you will surely be asked to represent your organization as a public speaker, to discuss your area of expertise, or to explain some program or policy your school or company has endorsed.

In spite of the inevitability of public speaking, many dread the thought of making a speech. Right now, for example, you may feel a lot of anxiety about even the idea of giving a speech. You may not know where to begin. How do you decide what to talk about? What can you realistically accomplish? Where can you go for information? How will you organize your thinking? How should you present your remarks? These are the kinds of questions that this book is designed to answer.

The purpose of *Basic Public Speaking* is to introduce to you the fundamentals of effective public communication. Although the communication process is complex, this book divides public speaking into several *manageable* content areas, such as choosing a purpose for your speech. Then, within each content area, I identify several specific objectives to be accomplished after reading and practicing the principles advocated in the chapter are identified. After studying each chapter and going through the exercises listed at the end, you can return to the objectives and decide to what extent you have been able to accomplish each one. Some of the objectives are more readily met than others. It is fairly easy, for example, to describe the kinds of speeches you might be asked to make as either a student or a professional person (Chapter 1). More difficult is devising strategies for overcoming your own communication barriers (Chapter 2). With practice and perseverance you can achieve the objectives presented in this book.

Basic Public Speaking also focuses on skills acquisition. However, it is not so much rules-based as it is grounded in *principles* of effective communication. Rather than asking you to do "these ten things" with the hope that you will become a good public speaker, you are asked to think of speechmaking in terms of your attitudes, fears, goals, and your ability to improve over time. Principles of strategy, flexibility, audience adaptation, and purpose awareness are stressed. In contrast to rigid rules, these communication principles can be applied flexibly in diverse situations. Thus, when you encounter sensitive subjects, apathetic audiences, or unrealistic time constraints, you will be better able to respond appropriately.

Finally, *Basic Public Speaking* presents public speaking skills in the context of a general understanding of the human communication process. Many of our problems as public speakers stem from our difficulties in daily communication. To be an excellent communicator in any situation requires an understanding of the process nature of communication, an awareness of potential communication barriers, many of which are rooted in our attitudes and prejudices, and sensitivity to the listening habits and worries of those to whom we speak. We begin this book with an examination of these issues as applied to the public speaking situation. Only when we recognize the tendencies, frailties, and expectations that all of us carry with us as we reach out to influence others can we hope to become good public communicators.

The book is divided into nine chapters. The first three set the stage for all that follow, providing a basic understanding of the nature of communication and potential communication problems, from the perspective of both the speaker and the audience. Chapter 4 turns to a specific consideration of speech anxiety, its nature, causes, symptoms, and some management strategies. The early treatment of this topic is designed to make you feel more comfortable with the idea of giving a speech before going on and tackling your first speech assignment. Chapters 5 through 9 systematically deal with each major step in the speech preparation process, including topic selection, purpose selection, finding supporting materials, organizing the speech, and delivering the speech. Particular emphasis is put on the notion of purpose since one's purpose as a public speaker influences every other decision about organization, delivery, and the use of evidence. The content of each chapter is broken into several manageable objectives toward which any speaker who is developing skills might strive.

Communicating with other people is probably one of the most important and meaningful things we do during our lives. As we try to communicate effectively with others, we are forced to confront our own weaknesses; we are also given the chance to develop our strengths. Most crucial personal, social, political, and business decisions are made by people who speak to one another, who listen to one another, and who ultimately choose where they stand. As public speakers we have the challenge and the chance to influence others to think, act, and believe as we feel they should. We also have the opportunity and the responsibility to listen, to learn, and to grow. Excellent public speakers are as good at listening to audiences and their concerns as they are at articulating their own beliefs. Like all forms of communication, public speaking is a give-and-take process.

I could not have completed this book without the concern, support, and inspiration of many, many people. I want to thank, first, my friends and colleagues at Indiana University who have provided an intellectual environment in which my writing was encouraged and appreciated. Special thanks are also extended to Louise Waller, my editor and my friend, who believed in this project and provided sound guidance throughout the writing process. I also extend my gratitude and love to my parents, Arthur and Helen Hayes, who consistently greet my writing projects with joy and admiration. To my husband, Jim, for whom loving support is a way of life, I extend my deepest thanks. Finally, it is my dear daughter, Jennifer Elizabeth, to whom I dedicate this book.

Patricia Bradley Andrews

chapter *1*

Public Speaking and the Communication Process

CHAPTER OBJECTIVES

After studying this chapter you should be able to:

1. Describe the kinds of speeches you might be asked to make as either a student or a professional.
2. Compare and contrast a traditional with a process view of communication.
3. Explain the ways in which public speaking might reflect a process orientation.

INTRODUCTION

You have been asked to make a speech. It all started when you were elected president of your student government. As president you came up with some interesting ideas about how to enhance your school's image by increasing public service activities and implementing higher academic standards. Your ideas worked, and the word has spread. Now the national president of NASCO, the National Association of Student Government Officers, has phoned you and asked you to speak at NASCO's annual convention, soon to be held in your state. The president tells you that you will be speaking to an audience of about 300, including the national board of directors, officers from all over the United States, and a few local political figures. She concludes by telling you that she is proud of you, that you are important to your college, and that she knows you will do a "dynamite" job of representing your college and its student government association. You begin to perspire.

Perhaps it seems that this scenario is strictly hypothetical and that it could never apply to you. You may imagine that the only people who have to make public speeches are professionals with significant, long-standing records of accomplishment. If this were the case, these people would do little more than make speeches, because there is such a great demand for public speakers. Not only do executives, ministers, and others with official leadership positions make speeches with some regularity, but so do lower level supervisors, students, and even rank-and-file workers. A recent survey of blue-collar workers in Albany, New York, for example, revealed that most had given at least one speech during the preceding two-year period (1). *This study also found that as the educational level of individuals climbed, so did the frequency of their public speaking activities.* The fact that you are studying for a college degree increases the likelihood that you will be asked to speak sometime in the future. You may have to make speeches in your career, for most professional people do so from time to time. These speeches may be delivered within the company or to some group outside of the organization. The audience may be very small or extremely large. The speeches may range from technical reports or staff briefings to eloquent manuscript presentations. Factors in the speaking situation may vary, but in one form or another, public speaking happens often.

There are numerous business, civic, religious, and social organizations that meet each month or even each week. For part of their meetings they need "programs." Their program directors typically invite outside speakers to share their experiences, ideas, or expertise. Many colleges and universities maintain student speakers' bureaus. These groups give students a chance to develop a 20- to 30-minute presentation on some subject in which they are interested or knowledgeable. Students may visit different community organizations that request speeches on topics of particular interest to them. In this context students are regularly invited to address such diverse groups as the PTA, the Lions Club, the United Methodist Women, the Rotary Club, the Accounting Club, and the League of Women Voters. Later, as business and professional people, some of you will be asked to speak for special events, such as high school commencements, convention luncheons, and political rallies.

Most audiences like to hear about a variety of topics, so they invite several different kinds of speakers to address them each year. They ask doctors to discuss open-heart surgery, students to discuss the advantages of studying abroad, lawyers to speak about divorce laws and capital punishment, and teachers to talk about dyslexia or reading enrichment programs. Social workers may be invited to discuss new casework techniques or blended families, while businesspeople are asked to talk about consumer trends, advertising practices, and investment opportunities. Whatever you know a great deal about, whatever you specialize in, that is the kind of subject you will likely be asked to discuss. The range of potential topics is great.

The instances of public speaking we have examined so far all involve an individual addressing a group of which he or she is not a member. Consider the scenario appearing at the beginning of this chapter for a moment. If you were in the position of being asked to make the speech described there, it would be usual for you to prepare your remarks a few days early and present them first to your own student government's executive board. This would give you a "dry run" while allowing your peers to hear what you plan to say.

Suppose you are an officer in the student honor society who has been asked to address the university's student council concerning plagiarism and cheating. Or imagine yourself a college professor explaining to a group of your colleagues the newly formulated policies of the College Curriculum Committee. Or you could be an architect about to present to a local school board alternative building plans for a new high school. These are only a few examples of proposal presentations and technical reports that occur regularly within organizations.

Of course, some business and professional people speak regularly as part of the daily course of their jobs. Ministers preach, teachers give lectures, attorneys make courtroom speeches, and sales representatives give sales talks. Perhaps the profession you plan to enter will require you to make frequent speeches. More likely, you will be asked to speak at least from time to time. Perhaps someone needs information which only you possess. Or maybe your company is having financial troubles and you are going to present a plan to bail them out. Possibly your organization needs some articulate person to represent them by speaking to an important community group.

Public speaking is important. You will not make speeches as often as you talk informally with your peers, or even as frequently as you participate in committee meetings. However, when you are asked or volunteer to make a speech, that will represent a significant communication event.

Of all the kinds of communicative exchanges we engage in, public speaking is among the most formal. *Effective public speaking requires careful attention to topic selection and focus, audience analysis, organization, content, and delivery.* It takes time to prepare a good speech. Those who assemble to listen to a speaker implicitly agree to give that speaker "the right" to talk until he or she has finished the presentation. Rarely are public speakers interrupted. As a public speaker you have an opportunity to discuss information and ideas you believe to be important, and to share with others those things you value, information you find provocative, or a plan you want them to accept. Public speaking provides you with a formal opportunity to exert influence, to enhance your own image, and to represent your school or organization. Thus, public speaking presents both challenge and responsibility.

OVERVIEW

This book introduces you to effective public speaking by examining the kinds of objectives you should develop and pursue as you plan, conduct research, organize, and deliver your speech. *Identifying objectives is a crucial initial step.* Once you know what you hope to accomplish, it is far easier to choose judiciously the techniques and strategies to get you there. At the beginning of each chapter you will find a list of general objectives, stating what you should be able to define, identify, distinguish, analyze, evaluate, or do by the time you have completed the chapter and its exercises. You may wish to add to these some of your own goals as you acquire public speaking skills. These objectives provide checkpoints to which you should refer often in order to judge your progress.

There are many different kinds of public speeches that you may be asked to give. To some extent, each speaking situation you encounter will be unique to you, your position (student or professional), and the needs of your audience. Some of you will take jobs that require you regularly to make technical reports to small groups of specialists within your company who understand the jargon of your profession and who desire an information-packed, highly technical presentation. Or you may speak to a more general group within your organization, perhaps managers representing manufacturing, financial, sales, personnel, and development concerns. Finally, many of you will make speeches to groups to which you do not belong. For students this is common. In these instances, you represent both your school and yourself. In a sense your speaking becomes a kind of public relations effort. In these situations you need to be interesting, clear, and careful that you reflect positively on those you represent.

Regardless of the particular kind of speech you make, many of the principles of effective public speaking are the same. *If you are speaking to a small group of students, you will do things differently than if you are presenting a formal manuscript speech before a Congressional hearing.* Yet, in both instances, you will pick and focus on a subject, select a purpose, choose a pattern of organization, seek supporting materials for your arguments or main points, and choose a style of delivery. *In adapting the speech to your audience you will deal with each of these aspects uniquely because both the audiences and the speaking occasions will be so different.* The extent to which you are able to match the needs of the speech situation with your treatment of the subject will largely determine your success.

Public speaking is only one kind of communication activity. To understand how to develop specific skills in public speaking it is important first to think about communication in general, to understand what the components of the communication process are, and to recognize the complexity of most communication interactions.

THE TRADITIONAL VIEW OF COMMUNICATION

Until two or three decades ago communication practitioners and theorists gave most of their attention to the role of the speaker in communication transactions, or exchanges. The speaker, they believed, had to make certain choices. He had to decide, for example, what topic to discuss, how to support his point of view, whether to use note cards or manuscript, and even how to dress. If he chose wisely, he would probably succeed. Poor choices and/or performance would lead to failure. *Early views of communication minimized the importance of the audience, focusing instead on the significance of the speaker.* In fact, the traditional view of communication was *linear* (see Figure 1.1). The message flow moved in one direction, from speaker to listeners, and listener response was ignored.

As you can see, the traditional model has four parts: *speaker, message,*

A TRADITIONAL, LINEAR MODEL OF COMMUNICATION

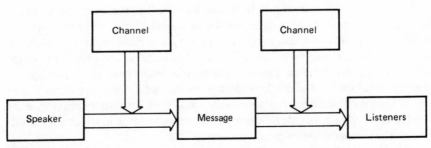

Figure 1.1

channel, and *listeners* (2). The speaker is the person who encodes the message; that is, she takes an idea and changes it into a symbol that she assumes represents some common meaning for both her and the audience. Her symbols are words. The more concrete the words, the more likely both speaker and audience will have a common understanding of their meaning. Most of us have commonly shared notions of tennis shoes, refrigerators, balloons, boxing gloves, and bulldogs. We are more likely, however, to have varying notions of what is meant by love, beauty, democracy, liberal politics, or power. Good speakers do not avoid using such abstract words, but they are careful either to place them in a context that clarifies their meaning or to provide definitions.

The second component in the traditional model is the message. We assume that whenever a speaker speaks, it is because she has something on her mind, something she believes to be worth communicating. That "something" is the message. The communicated message includes more than the words of the speech. Messages are both verbal and nonverbal, intentional and unintentional. However carefully we select our words, the complete message we send will also be determined by our posture, gestures, facial expression, eye contact, and tone of voice. A speaker might point out, for example, "That's an interesting idea." If she stresses "that's" and sounds enthusiastic, we will assume she is genuinely enthusiastic about the idea. But she might make the same statement with a tone of sarcasm and derision, and we conclude that she is against the idea. The words are the same; the message is different. Many nonverbal messages are intentional, planned by the speaker to create an effect. Others are unintentional. We have all seen speakers who act nervous while claiming to be calm, or who sound bored while mouthing words of commitment. *Clearly, the intended message and the received message are not always the same because the nonverbal communication may "conflict" with the spoken words.*

Messages must be transmitted in some manner. The mode or method of transmission is the channel. Normally when we envision a public speaker we think of his vocal mechanism as the primary communication channel. Certainly the voice is a major communication channel, but so too are the face, the hands, and, in fact, the whole body. So far, we have focused on channels in the most personal sense; that is, channels associated with the speaker himself. Often, however, more impersonal channels play an important role. Sometimes a speaker must decide whether he will use a microphone or rely on his own vocal projection. The microphone will help him to be heard, but it will also change the quality of his voice. Microphones have been known to squeak, hum, and overamplify a speaker's voice; any of these things can be very annoying to an audience. On occasion a speaker may be asked to deliver a message on television or over the radio. Both communication channels are very different from the typical public speaking situation. Gestures are irrelevant on the radio, for example, but one's tone of voice and vocal expressiveness are vital. With television speaking, one's mobility is usually restricted and close-ups create a condition in which eye contact and facial expression are of prime concern.

Finally, speakers have to decide whether or not to release their remarks to the press after they speak. Since in this instance the written manuscript as well as the delivered speech will be judged, the speaker must take great pains with sentence structure and word choice. *Clearly, the speaker must be concerned with the channel or message medium as well as with the speech itself.*

The final component in the traditional speech communication model is the audience, or listeners. The traditional view places listeners on the receiving end. They receive the message in a passive way, and any response they make is ignored by the model. Somehow, when the speaker has finished, we get the feeling that nothing else remains except for everyone to go home. Such a view of communication, while rather neat and orderly, is scarcely realistic. Listeners do respond. They have likes and dislikes. They judge and they misjudge. They feel inspired and they become confused. Perhaps the easiest way to acknowledge audience response is to add a simple feedback loop to our original traditional model (see Figure 1.2). This addition creates a cyclical model rather than a linear one and is more realistic.

The skilled speaker makes every attempt to *monitor* audience feedback. As she monitors, she goes through several steps:

A COMMUNICATION MODEL WITH FEEDBACK LOOP

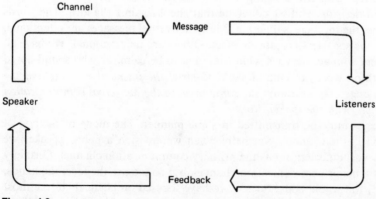

Figure 1.2

1. *Watching* for some audience response. (For example, audience members smiling.)
2. *Interpreting* the feedback. (What does it mean when the audience smiles? Approval? Ridicule?)
3. *Analyzing* the response. (Why did the response occur? What caused it?)
4. *Responding* to the feedback. (For example, questioning, adapting, or plodding on.

As you can see, the monitoring process requires the speaker to be alert, perceptive, and committed to being responsive.

In viewing the model (Figure 1.2) it is important to recall that feedback is not the same as audience response. Traditionally they are seen as closely related, but they are not the same.

Imagine yourself seated in an audience during a public speech. The speaker has a high-pitched nasal voice and she is talking about the need for a new gymnasium to better serve both the school your younger sister attends and the community at large. You don't really agree with her. Your sister is a musician, and the school's music facilities and auditorium are wonderful. Besides, your sister loathes sports (as do you). Yet, you are a polite listener and you sit attentively with your eyes fixed on the speaker. Perhaps you even smile from time to time, and nod your head as if in agreement. (After all, this woman is your family's neighbor and your mother works with her in the PTA.) Clearly in this instance your response (which is negative) and your feedback (which is positive) are not the same. *Your feedback is the portion of your response that you send back to the speaker.*

Feedback can be either verbal or nonverbal. Usually it is both. If you are confused, you may frown, squirm, and raise your hand to ask a question. If you are disgusted with a speaker's comments, you may whisper to your neighbor, throw the speaker a hostile stare, and huff up after the speech to give the speaker a piece of your mind. All of these are feedback responses.

What is important to recall is that the speaker can only do something about the responses you let her see. If you are confused and hide it, don't expect the speaker to provide clarification. If you disagree but refuse to voice your dissent, there is no hope for you and the speaker to achieve a common understanding. All listeners respond. Most provide feedback. Some provide genuine feedback. Genuine feedback is the kind most likely to have a positive impact on the outcome of the total communication process.

COMMUNICATION AS PROCESS

In 1960, communication scholar David Berlo published a book entitled *The Process of Communication* (3). In it he argued that all communication, including public speaking, should be viewed from a process perspective. Why should this be necessary? What do we mean by "communication as process"? First, we need a process view of communication because traditional views of communication are oversimplified. They consider too few of the components present in actual communication transactions. In that sense, their utility is limited. Second, early views of communication were static. They assumed that the speaker made a speech (that is, communicated *one* message) and the listener reacted (that is, made *one* response). Multiple messages and varying responses were ignored. Finally, the traditional view of communication overemphasized the role of the speaker. Listeners played a minor role; their responses, when considered, were viewed as far less important than the speaker's message.

Perhaps the major problem with the traditional view of communication was the extent to which it emphasized the source or speaker. Among other things, it assumed that the speaker was in complete control of the message outcome. This is scarcely the case. In many ways the speaker is like the owner of a business. Anyone who has ever owned or managed his own business soon learns that although he is, technically speaking, the boss, and in that sense is in charge, his success as a businessman depends in large measure upon whether or not he pleases his customers. He has to understand their whims, tastes, moods, needs, and interests. The way he treats them is almost as important as the quality of the car, shirt, meat, or ice skates he is selling. If he knows them well it helps. If they know him it helps (that is, assuming they trust and like him). He soon learns that however wonderful he believes his product to be, whatever his reasons for liking it, what he really needs to figure out are the kinds of products his customers will find appealing.

Clearly, there are many similarities between selling a product and arguing a point of view. Most important is that both salesperson and customer, both speaker and listener, have control over the outcome of the persuasive transaction. A product which seems palatable only to the person selling it will not find a buyer. Neither will an idea that is appealing only to the speaker find a receptive audience. *Speakers share control with listeners.* Every stage in the speech preparation process should reflect an understanding of that fact.

When I speak of communication as process, I am acknowledging several points. First, in the spirit of the preceding paragraph, communication is *transactional;* it involves the exchange of messages. The speaker and the listener may also exchange roles from time to time, even in the context of a formal public speech. For example, the speaker says, "I would never get an abortion, no matter what." The listener raises an eyebrow, frowns, looks skeptical (as if to say, "Really? Under no circumstance would you consider it?). In this instance both listener and speaker have sent messages. Because the listener's was nonverbal and hence ambiguous, we could only guess at what he was thinking, but his nonverbal behavior clearly indicated that he questioned the speaker's assertion. We cannot argue that one message is more important than the other, or that only the speaker's is a "true" message simply because he is the speaker. Because communication is transactional, ideas are raised, questioned, defended, rebutted, or accepted in this interchange of messages. Through speaker-listener interaction the communication outcome is determined.

When we begin to understand communication as process, we also start to recognize that it is *dynamic;* it is in a state of flux. As speakers and listeners act and react, send and receive, many things happen. At the beginning of your speech

A speaker listens to someone asking him a question. This act shows the transactional process of communication. (Photo courtesy of Arthur Grace, Stock, Boston.)

you may feel positive. Later you may feel nervous because you are starting to discuss the part of your plan you believe to be most controversial. Still later, you may become confident and enthusiastic as the audience laughs with you or applauds a point you've made. What is important is that all of these may happen to you during a single speech.

One reason your feelings vary as you speak is because your listeners' reactions vary as well. They may be mildly bored, amused, excited, and confused at different points during your speech. If a psychologist were to measure their blood pressure or Galvanic Skin Response (a measure of excitement) during your speech, those too would most likely vary. Hence, communication is dynamic. It does not begin "here" and end "there" with nothing of note transpiring in between. Rather, it is a living thing. It grows, changes, influences, and is influenced. During a 30-minute speech many different responses will occur from both sides of the podium. Rarely does a speaker feel totally positive or negative about his or her speechmaking. Rarely does an audience completely endorse or reject a speaker's ideas. And the speech really doesn't end when speaker and audience go home. As they continue to think, analyze, reflect, and engage others in a dialogue about the speech's subject, the communication process continues.

Finally, a process view of communication recognizes that each speech communication event is unique. No matter how many times you practice your speech, no matter how similar your audiences may be, each communication transaction is an event unto itself; it can never be replicated. Even if you join a speaker's bureau and present the same speech over and over again, you will still encounter many varying factors each time. Your feelings, the audience's response, and the physical environment are three obvious variables.

The uniqueness of public communication is part of what makes it very special—special in two ways: First, each speaking situation is different, hence, a challenge. How dull it would be if you could anticipate everything in advance! Second, and equally important, as a unique event each public speech should be valued as something that can be remembered, discussed, condemned, or savored, but as something that can never be recreated. Communication is, after all, an act of human creativity. At public speaking events we recognize that fact in a rather formal way. As audience members we sit and listen to another's thoughts, trying to follow his line of thinking, striving to comprehend not just his point of view but his world view, the larger value scheme which frames his speech.

Similarly, as speakers, we choose the subject, we examine our audiences, we frame our arguments, we seek compelling support, we play with sentence structure and word choice, and we practice. *As public communicators we are called to use some of our most significant human talents and skills,* for we must be able to describe and analyze problems, to examine the strengths and weaknesses of alternative points of view, to search for compelling arguments, to find bright, clear language in which to express our ideas, and to view our audiences and the problems we face with compassion and sensitivity. If we are to succeed as public speakers we must be capable of moving outside ourselves to observe and comprehend the ways others think and feel. Such understanding will assist us in framing arguments that make sense to our audiences, ones that speak to their needs and values. Of course, effective communication is no trivial task. Understanding something about the nature of the communication process is only the beginning.

EXERCISES

1. Choose any organization in your home or school community. Find out whether or not it has any kind of speech training program. If it does, seek responses to the following questions:

   a. How long has the program been in operation?
   b. What does it entail?
   c. Who teaches it?
   d. Who is eligible/required to take it?
   e. What skills are stressed?
   f. Has it been evaluated? If so, how was it rated?
   g. What are your suggestions for changes/improvements?

   If the organization you selected lacks such a program, respond to the following:

   a. What kinds of speeches do individuals in this organization make?
   b. How many employees are asked to make speeches?
   c. How would they feel about having some training in public speaking?
   d. What kinds of skills might they desire to learn?
   e. Who might teach the course?

2. Make a list of the things you want to learn about public speaking. What speaking skills are you especially interested in improving? What do you presently consider to be your strengths as a speaker?

3. Construct your own model of communication using the public speaking situation as a frame of reference. Your model should include all key components in the communication process. Decide whether your model is traditional or process oriented. Justify the components you've included in your model. Could your model also be used to examine communication behavior in small group or interpersonal settings?

4. Write a paragraph in which you respond to the following question: What is an effective communicator?

Then write another paragraph in which you address this question: What is an effective public speaker?

Keep these responses so that you may consult them after you have finished working through the exercises in this book.

NOTES

1. K. E. Kendall, "Do Real People Ever Give Speeches?" *Central States Speech Journal* 25 (1974), p. 233.

2. See for example, C. E. Shannon and W. Weaver, *The Mathematical Theory of Communication* (Urbana, Illinois: University of Illinois Press, 1949).

3. David Berlo, *The Process of Communication* (New York: Rinehart and Winston, 1960).

chapter *2*

Overcoming Barriers to Effective Communication

CHAPTER OBJECTIVES

After studying this chapter you should be able to:

1. Identify factors contributing to perceptual screening.
2. Explain the difference between fact and inference.
3. Identify stereotypes associated with yourself and with other groups of people.
4. Distinguish denotative from connotative meaning, listing appropriate examples.
5. Recognize that language creates social reality.
6. Identify additional factors that function as communication barriers for you.
7. Devise strategies for overcoming your communication barriers.

INTRODUCTION

Imagine yourself sitting in an audience listening to a speaker talk about the advantages of purchasing a particular type of automobile insurance. The speaker happens to be an attractive blonde. Although she seems to know what she is talking about, you find yourself wondering whether you really trust a woman's advice on this particular subject.

Now picture yourself in a different kind of audience situation. It is Monday morning and you and approximately 200 other students have just arrived for your 9:30 geology class. As your professor convenes the class and begins to discuss two recent theories of earth formation, you find yourself having difficulty concentrating on his remarks. He has the annoying habit of incessantly stroking his beard as he talks. This morning he seems to be curling it around his fingers and stretching it out as if to encourage its growth. Before you know it, he has moved on to discuss an impending examination and you have to ask someone after class if you can borrow her notes.

Finally, imagine that you are addressing the local chapter of Business and Professional Women about consumer buying behavior, a subject about which you have collected extensive information in your basic speech course. In discussing food purchasing habits you point out, "Most consumers shop in great haste. You ladies, for example, probably do most of the grocery shopping for your families. You're busy and you try to work your shopping around transporting your kids to and from school, meetings, and social gatherings. Or maybe you have to take the kids with you. They, of course, have ways of appealing to you to buy every item of junk food the store has to sell. In either case, you girls want to hurry and get the shopping over with." As you watch the audience, you sense you have said something wrong. What did you say that "turned them off"?

Each of these scenarios has something in common: they all describe common communication barriers. Perhaps right now you cannot readily identify them, but as you read further you will be able to recognize the problems they represent. You might have noticed already, for example, that the scenarios depict people having trouble both as speakers and as listeners. In Chapter 1 we pointed out that both parties, speakers and listeners, share control over the outcome of any communication transaction. They also share the responsibility for it. Even so, the road to effective communication is fraught with numerous hazards, barriers that prevent speakers and listeners from understanding and accepting one another.

COMMON COMMUNICATION BARRIERS

We cannot treat all potential communication barriers in this chapter, but we will discuss several of the most common and significant ones, including perceptual screening, failure to distinguish fact from inference, stereotyping, believing that meaning resides in words, and ignorance of the social reality created by language. In Figure 2.1, these communication barriers appear as a stone wall separating speaker from listener.

Perceptual Screens

If you have ever made a speech you know that from time to time someone in the audience will make a comment or ask a question that leads you to believe that person has missed your point completely. You may assume that the individual didn't listen to you, is exceptionally stupid, or is trying to antagonize you (and you may be right on all three counts). The chances are equally good, however, that he didn't receive your intended message because of perceptual screening. Such screening refers to factors within the listener—his experiences,

COMMUNICATION BARRIERS: THE WALL THAT SEPARATES

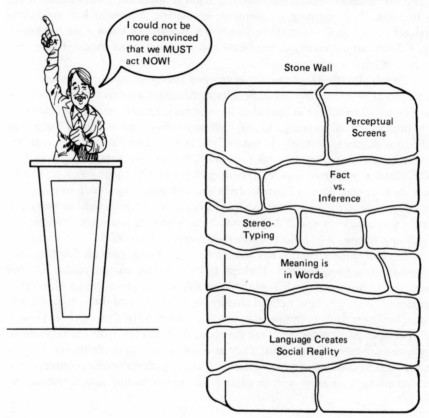

Figure 2.1

mindset, values, etc.—which interfere with his reception of your intended message.

Long before communication scholars recognized the existence of perceptual screens, they acknowledged the presence of "noise factors." This refers to such physical annoyances as poor acoustics, squeaky microphones, screaming children, or disturbances in the hallway. Since noise factors are tangible, they normally need only to be anticipated to be controlled or eliminated. Perceptual screens, in contrast, are more elusive. Often the screening process is automatic. Even the listener doesn't know he's doing it. Of course, some perceptual screening is inevitable. Our worlds are dynamic, complex, and ever-changing. None of us can fully perceive our surroundings. Like the child who goes to Disney World for a single afternoon in hopes of "talking it all in," we too will be disappointed if we fail to recognize some of our perceptual limitations.

Perceptual screens come in many forms. Sometimes we screen what a speaker says because we find it threatening. Suppose that on the first day of your required history course the professor states that, due to a mix-up at computer registration, too many students have been enrolled in his class. Unless different room arrangements can be made there is a chance that about 10 percent will have to drop the class. Then he goes on to explain the criteria that will be used in determining who will be asked to drop, should such procedures become necessary. Of course, you feel threatened since you are a graduating senior and the class is a requirement. Your feelings in this instance may cause you to screen the message in several different ways. First, you may distort what you've heard, dismissing the part of the message which indicated that the necessity of dropping was as yet uncertain. In your mind you are already standing in the drop-and-add lines. Moreover, because you feel insecure, you ignore your professor's statistics indicating class drops of only 10 percent. Stated another way, that means that 90 percent of you are safe! You, however, focus on the negative side of the situation. Finally, because you are so upset by your instructor's initial announcement, you fail to hear his discussion of the criteria to be used in determining who can remain in the class. Thus, you have filtered out precisely the kind of information you most need to allow you to plan judiciously for your own future.

Not everyone distorts messages in the manner just described. Some, for example, react with denial. They cope with unsettling news by minimizing the threat. In their minds, 10 percent is reduced to "a slight chance that a couple of students will be asked to leave." These listeners probably don't pay attention to the criteria either, for fear they might gain some information that would make their denial impossible. You may be thinking that denial sounds like a pretty strange and rather uncommon manner of coping with unpleasant news. On the contrary, most of us allow denial to affect our perceptions of what speakers really are saying. To speeches on the hazards of smoking, the threat of rape, the dangers of driving after drinking, and the risk of heart attack from overeating we often respond by reasoning, "It'll never happen to me!" In this manner we do not have to grapple with the personal implications of speakers' messages.

Our specific method of perceptual screening will vary as we move through different situations, listen to different speakers, and are exposed to new topics. Often, for example, we focus on those aspects of speeches that please us most. We want to hear what we perceive as reinforcing, confirming, and in agreement with our previously held views. On other occasions we look for inconsistencies. We are interested in comparing our views with those of others, with a mind toward reconciling differences. Thus, we skim over the commonalities and focus on the points of contrast. Newly married couples often experience this latter phenomenon, having gone through a marvelous courtship in which they believed they had everything in common, only to discover after the marriage ceremony that they are not exactly alike. These newly perceived differences may become a source of great consternation. The tendencies just described represent polarized approaches to perceiving other people's views. A middle ground is preferable, where both commonalities and differences are acknowledged in a realistic and less defensive light.

What we perceive of another's message will also depend upon our expectations and the role relationship existing between us. If you expect a speaker to be profound, you may perceive her as profound, regardless of the mundane comments she might make. If, in contrast, you anticipate that a speaker will be "a loser," you may find yourself incapable of appreciating anything of value she might say. Of course, whenever expectations are too high, we run the risk of dooming the speaker to failure. Most of us have had the experience of hearing that a particular speaker is "great," "fantastic," or "incredible." We attend the speech expecting to encounter the "Messiah" only to find a human being who is something less than perfect. Not only are we disappointed, but we fail to appreciate and learn from those qualities of excellence that gained the speaker her reputation in the first place.

Finally, the kinds of perceptual screens you construct will be determined in part by your previous experiences, values, and biases. If you believe, for example, that any woman who swears in public is not "a lady" and could not have anything of value to say to you, then you will probably refuse to hear the remarks of a female speaker who engages in such practices. We refer to this process as *abstracting,* that is, focusing on one aspect of a speaker's message or appearance and ignoring the others. The point of focus may vary; it may be an objectionable idea, poor grammar, vulgar language, poor organization, a questionable source, or even a peculiar hair style. Whatever the particular focal point, it becomes the organizing principle for all else that we perceive. Abstracting results in a perceptual process that usually reinforces existing biases. Another common perceptual problem is *bypassing.* Bypassing occurs whenever the speaker and the listener have a different frame of reference. The speaker intends one meaning and the listener interjects another. This becomes the grounds for further misunderstanding. The speaker, for example, talks of erotic materials and is really referring to great literary passages and fine works of art. The listener, on the other hand, translates "erotic materials" as pornographic movies and magazines. Almost any abstract term is a candidate for bypassing.

As a public speaker it is important that you be aware of perceptual screening. However, you cannot eliminate it; it is a factor in every speech occasion. But you can begin by looking at your audience and asking: Where might I be misunderstood? How can I make myself clearer? What examples might I use to give us a common frame of reference? Is there anything about my speech or language or appearance that might be distracting? How might I reduce the threat accompanying this message? As you seek the answers to these kinds of questions, you will begin to discover techniques for preventing perceptual screening from barring your attempts at effective communication.

Fact or Inference

Often as public speakers we believe that if we are to say anything of real worth, if we are to demonstrate our competence, we must present abundant facts. Somehow we believe that factual information will be better received and therefore our audiences will like us and our ideas more. Yet, consider the dictionary definitions of "fact": "something known with certainty . . . something that has been objectively verified . . . something having real, demonstrable existence" (1). Some subjects lend themselves well to a relatively factual treatment. The physical sciences, for example, are filled with facts one might share with an audience. Suppose, however, that you are discussing such value-laden, controversial issues as school closings, nuclear energy, social security reductions, or genetic engineering. With these kinds of topics, you as a speaker will most likely take a position, that is, you will argue for the endorsement of your point of view. Your position will be based on different kinds of evidence, including testimony, personal experience, statistics, and comparisons. Some of these will have a strong factual base; others cannot be verified in any objective way. Much of the time the ideas you advocate or the courses of action you support will be based as much on what seems to be most sensible as on what is correct in the factual sense.

Whenever we reach conclusions on the basis of our observations, we are making inferences. We see the doctor's car parked in front of our home and we infer or assume that someone is ill. Perhaps the doctor has stopped to ask for directions or his car has broken down and he is using the phone to call for help. But if we were betting, we would bet that someone is sick, possibly seriously so. That explanation seems more sensible, more likely. Since inferences involve mental leaps from observation to conclusion, they are probable, not absolute. As such, they are not the same as facts.

One cannot escape making inferences: both speakers and listeners make them with great regularity. In fact, without our ability to make inferences, we would not be able to function as reasoning human beings. Even so, it is crucial that public speakers distinguish fact from inference. As a reasoned conclusion, an inference represents our best judgment about what is correct, real, or worthy of our support. For example, after having carefully researched the school systems in a particular community, a concerned citizen might advocate that the school board close a particular elementary school based on its spare enrollment and its need for immediate renovation. He may well be correct in concluding that closing this school is the preferred course of action. What is important to recall about inferences, however, is that there is always some room for error. Even our most sophisticated inferential statistics are based on samples and therefore involve probabilities. That means that there is some chance, however remote, that the speaker could be mistaken. There might be a negative factor of which he is unaware. For example, it is possible that closing this school would result in placing students into already overcrowded schools, thus creating a different kind of problem.

Clearly, all reasoned conclusions should be approached with some tentativeness. Even with sound research and excellent thinking going into a proposal, there is always a chance that something has been overlooked. The speaker who is tentative in his advocacy is perfectly safe in saying, "I have studied this problem for weeks and I am convinced . . ." or "Having worked for this company for thirty years I feel I can say with confidence . . . ." But that is not the same as saying, "I know I am right. There is no other way. I will not budge." While few speakers make these kinds of definitive assertions, many succeed in communicating an attitude that is so dogmatic and rigid, there can be little doubt in the audience's mind that this speaker views herself as the "fount of all knowledge." Audiences enjoy speakers who are knowledgeable, competent, and confident. One can be all

Looking at this woman, observers can make several inferences. They can infer that she is shouting because she is angry, is loudly conveying information, or is in pain. (Photo courtesy of Paul Sequeira, Photo Researchers, Inc.)

of these things, however, without also being dogmatic and closed-minded. Although audiences spend a good deal of their time listening, they usually like to feel that there remains some mutual openness between them and the speaker, that their comments might be welcomed, and that their willingness to be influenced might be reciprocated.

Stereotyping

See if you can solve the following riddle:

> A father and his son were driving along the highway when the father suddenly
> lost control of the car and crashed into a telephone pole. The father was killed

instantly and his son was badly injured. The boy was rushed to the local hospital where it was found that he was suffering from serious internal injuries. A prominent surgeon was immediately summoned. When the surgeon arrived and went to the operating room to examine the boy, a loud gasp was heard. "I can't operate on this boy," the surgeon said. "He is my son."(2)

What is the solution? The father is dead; how could the boy be the surgeon's son?

Actually, the answer is quite straightforward. The surgeon is a woman and is also the boy's mother. If you have never heard this riddle before, you probably had some difficulty figuring it out. In fact, recent research has demonstrated that among those who had not heard the story previously, only 3 out of 26 males and 4 out of 24 females were able to answer it correctly (3). What is interesting, however, is that when the riddle is changed slightly so that the surgeon is described as bursting into tears and becoming hysterical upon seeing the boy, many more individuals are able to solve it correctly (4). Apparently these extra clues, which are consistent with widely held stereotypes about women, are sufficient to suggest the correct response.

Stereotypes of women abound, as do stereotypes of Jews, blacks, men, college students, ministers, lawyers, and professors. Men, for example, are thought to be strong, forceful, in control, aggressive, and self-reliant. Women, in contrast, are believed to be emotional, tender, dependent, submissive, and meek. While some of our stereotypes are changing, stereotyping remains a serious barrier to effective communication.

The dictionary defines "stereotype" as "a person, group, event, or issue considered to typify or conform to any unvarying pattern or manner, lacking any individuality (5)." Stereotyping is an extension of our inductive reasoning process in that we observe a few of a particular category (for example, mothers, Catholics, accountants, two-year-olds, Democrats, or actresses) and we draw conclusions about others belonging to the same category. *The difference between making a generalization about a group of individuals and stereotyping them is that when we stereotype we leave no room for individual differences.* As the definition above suggests, we believe that each individual will fit the mental mold we have fashioned with unvarying regularity.

Stereotyping interferes with effective communication from both sides of the podium. Sometimes the audience stereotypes the speaker: "Oh, he's a typical Republican" or "She's a feminist." Similarly, the speaker may make stereotypic judgments about the audience: "They're just an average church group" or "What can you say to a group of women about the economy?" Often we make stereotypic judgements based on minimal information. We may know, for example, someone's political affiliation, sex, age, or religion. But that is only the beginning. We need to know more.

At some time in our lives, nearly all of us stereotype. Our reasons for doing it vary. Often we stereotype because we are lazy. We don't want to worry about the complexity of each human being and so we find it more convenient to notice a few details and jump to a quick conclusion. On other occasions we may stereotype because we are insecure. We want to be able to predict other people's response patterns and we feel more certain of those when we can say, "Oh, I know his type!" Finally, stereotyping represents for many an unconscious process. We aren't aware that we are doing anything "wrong"; we've simply learned to respond to other individuals in quick and general ways.

In examining our own stereotyping behavior, it is useful to begin by thinking of ourselves on the receiving end of other people's stereotypes. How does it feel? Reflect on the stereotypes that could be applied to you. Make a list of your personal qualities, job affiliations, etc., that could be stereotyped. What is the stereotype associated with each? More important, in what ways do you believe you differ from the stereotype? Use the chart appearing in Table 2.1 to fill in your responses. Hopefully, in filling out the stereotype chart, you have gained some of these kinds of insights:

1. Stereotypes abound.
2. It is easier to think about stereotyping someone else than it is to examine the extent to which we ourselves may be stereotyped.
3. Most stereotypes have some truth to them. You probably found that you have some things in common with your own stereotypic description of the "typical man" (or woman).
4. All stereotypes have something wrong with them. Your variations from the stereotype were at least as great as your commonalities.

In all communication situations, and public speaking is no exception, we need to be sensitive to the uniqueness of each person we meet. Audiences are composed of individuals. A speaker represents himself, as well as IBM, Indiana University, or the Presbyterian Church. Far more important than classifying a speaker is understanding him. Later we can consider how he is similar to or different from others. Perhaps at that point we can make generalizations or render judgments. What is essential first, however, is that we consider the merit of the speaker's ideas as expressions of his unique perspective.

Table 2.1 STEREOTYPING CHART: SELF-ANALYSIS

Your personal quality	The common stereotype	How you think you differ
(Examples provided)		
1. College professor	Aloof, superior, head in the clouds, boring	Warm, friendly, interested in students
2. Single parent	Swinging, slightly irresponsible, unstable, often depressed	Responsible, tired, frustrated, loving
3. Methodist	Bible-beating Christian, methodical approach to religion	Flexible religious views
4. Woman	Emotional, meek, dependent, tender, passive	Active, emotional, rational, tender, loving
5. (another appropiate personal characteristic)		

Assuming That Meaning Is in Words

Words are symbols. We use them to represent our ideas, feelings, and points of view. With them we point to persons, places, objects, and concepts. By using words we are able to communicate some of our ideas. We can share them with others, perhaps to inform them, to amuse them, or to convince them of the reality or validity of our ideas. Whether we communicate successfully will depend in large measure upon the extent to which what we mean by a word is similar to what the receiver means by the word. Notice that the meaning resides in the communicator, not in the words. Of course, meanings cannot be assigned arbitrarily. Accepted meanings evolve as language develops. But even within the framework of accepted meanings there is still room for considerable diversity.

Consider the fact that in daily conversation the average adult uses about 2000 out of the 600,000 words available to him or her in the English language. Of these 2000, the 500 most common ones have over 14,000 dictionary definitions! Equally important, dictionary definitions normally represent denotative meaning, that is, meaning that is fairly standard, descriptive, operational, and perhaps scientific. What happens, however, when a speaker begins to tell you about "home," "love," "truth," "patriotism," "God," "poverty," or "trust"? These words deal not just with objective reality but with one's experience. We say that their meaning is connotative, rich with thought, feeling, experience, and ideas. The meaning we give these words will depend in large measure upon our experiences and observations. Some of us, for example, equate "patriotism" with "good citizenship." Others think of men marching off to war. Still others may think of the Archie Bunker stereotype, the bigot who hates all minorities, who hangs out his flag on Flag Day but knows nothing of courage or sacrifice.

The point is that words are not magic; they do not automatically signify in the minds of others what we hope or intend. *As effective public speakers we must create a context in which our meaning is made clear.* We can do this through examples, illustrations, visual materials, definitions, and explanations. Sometimes we can specify or suggest our intended meaning nonverbally. If we say the word "patriotism" with a warm smile and a voice of respect, we suggest a positive association. A tone of sarcasm or derision would imply the opposite. What is important is that we recognize the need for creating clear images and common frames of reference in the receivers' minds. The words we choose, the context in which we place them, the examples we use to illuminate them, the definitions we give them, and the way we say them will all contribute to our receivers' understanding of what we, in fact, mean.

Forgetting That Language Creates Social Reality

Consider the following list:

Blot
Blight
Smut

Murky
Threatening
Foreboding
Sinister
Evil
Malignant
Unwashed
Foul

These are listed as synonyms for a commonly used word in a popular thesaurus. What do you think that word is? It may not surprise you to learn that the word is "black." If you continue to look through this same thesaurus, you will discover some other interesting lists of synonyms. For example, "yellow" is associated with coward, timid, spiritless, sneak, and lily-livered whereas "white" is synonymous with purity, cleanliness, chaste, innocent, honorable, genuine, and just (6). Maybe you are thinking that those kinds of associations are fairly common ones, quite representative of how these words are used and what they, in fact, mean. If that is the case in any objective sense, we should be able to collect similar lists of synonyms for these words in other languages. We might begin by going to a Chinese dictionary. There we would find that "yellow" is synonymous with beauty, flowering, and sunshine whereas "white" suggests coldness, frigidity, bloodlessness, and weakness. Moreover, in some African tongues, "black" connotes strength, certainty, and integrity; "white," however, is defined as pale, anemic, and devious (7). The racial associations are obvious.

　　Clearly, the "meanings" of these words change radically as we examine them in different cultures. These changes do not occur by chance alone. Rather, the "meanings" of these words reflect the values, biases, attitudes, and feelings of the people who use them. When we use words that reveal our prejudices and values, we are also reaching out to influence the attitudes of others. Sometimes this process is largely unconscious. On other occasions, we choose our words with a greater sense of persuasive purpose. The point to remember, however, is that language is not a neutral medium of social exchange. Our language has evolved in ways that reveal who we are, what we value, and how we think others should view the world.

COMMUNICATION BARRIERS IN PERSPECTIVE

It would be nice if, at the end of this chapter, you would find a list entitled, "Do These Ten Things And Your Communication Barriers Will Vanish." Such a simplistic treatment of communication barriers, unfortunately, is not possible. First, some of the phenomena I have discussed are inevitable, such as perceptual screening and making inferences. These have to be recognized and managed, but they cannot, and indeed should not, be eliminated. Moreover, most of these processes represent enduring habitual patterns, ways we have been taught or have learned to deal with our social environments. We stereotype, for example, because we need to feel secure in our dealings with others. We screen threatening information because we want to feel comfortable and safe. Perceptual screening probably gives us false security, but it may take us a while to recognize that fact. So, when we examine perceptual screening, stereotyping, confusing facts with inferences, or attributing meaning to words rather than to people, we are looking at long-standing habits, patterns of interaction, and psychological coping devices. They will not disappear because you have read this chapter.

What, then, might you aim to achieve? First, you need an awareness of communication barriers and an understanding of their basic nature and function. Hopefully, at this point, you have both awareness and understanding. Next, you need to examine your own communication behavior (both as speaker and as receiver) and determine the extent to which these barriers represent problems for you. Ask yourself the following questions:

1. Do I screen information in consistent ways? How? What do I seem to be missing as a result of it?
2. To what extent do I react to and treat others in stereotypic ways? Are there any particular kinds of people for whom I hold strong stereotypes?
3. Do I ever treat inferences as facts? What opinions do I hold so strongly that I tend to view them as facts? Are there any arguments that might be advanced to refute these views? What are they?
4. Are there any words which I use in ways peculiar to me and/or my family and friends? What words might I use in speeches that would need to be defined or clarified? How would I define them or make them clear?
5. What are some words that have very strong value associations? Do I ever use these words? How might I eliminate some of them or use them more responsibly?

Responses to the above questions should generate a more specific awareness of your own communication tendencies. Finally, as enduring human interaction patterns, the barriers identified in this chapter are phenomena with which most of us will grapple throughout our lives. As we strive to stereotype less, distinguish fact from inference, and perceive more completely, the quality of our communication interactions should improve substantially. But just as the pianist must practice daily or risk losing his skills, we too must work with these barriers in a continuing way. *Becoming an effective communicator is not so much a goal one achieves as a process with which one works.*

EXERCISES

1. The next time you go to listen to a speech, take along a tape recorder. With the speaker's permission, record his or her speech. Immediately after listening to the speech, jot down what you believe to be the speaker's main ideas and/or anything that strikes you as being worthy of your remembering. Then take home the tape and listen to it once or twice. List any main points or significant concepts you omitted after initially listening to the oral presentation. What kinds of things did you omit or distort? Were they things with which you agreed or disagreed? How strong was the speaker's evidence supporting ideas with which you disagreed? Did you recall any of that evidence after the initial hearing? Are there any conclusions you might draw about your own patterns of perceptual screening?

2. Consider the following list of some groups that are commonly stereotyped. Describe what you believe to be the stereotype associated with each. Then, for each grouping listed, give one example of an individual you have known who does not fit the stereotype.

> Women
> Men
> Blacks
> Jews
> Football players
> Accountants
> Lawyers
> Secretaries
> Factory workers
> School teachers

3. Look up the following words in a good dictionary. List two or three dictionary (denotative) definitions for each. Then write a paragraph in which you discuss what these words mean to you and what experiences you have had which have helped form your notions of these terms (connotative meanings).

> Love
> Poor
> Patriotic
> Communism
> Educated
> Political
> Religious

4. Read the following story as many times as you like. Then cover it up and respond to the questions that follow it. Don't allow yourself to consult the story until you are completely finished with the questions.

The woman had just flipped on the lights and seated herself behind the desk when the bell rang. Students came pouring into the room, chattering among themselves. Suddenly a man appeared. He demanded that she empty her purse. After the purse was emptied, the man left abruptly. The woman quickly notified the police.

In responding to these questions, mark you answers as follows:

T = True, stated as fact in the story.
F = False, positively disconfirmed by the story.
? = You cannot say for sure, in the factual sense, based on the story.

1. The woman in this story was a school teacher.	T	F	?
2. The robbery occured at night.	T	F	?
3. The robber was a man.	T	F	?
4. The robber was one of the students.	T	F	?
5. The woman was seated behind the desk when the bell rang.	T	F	?

6. The bell was a fire alarm.   T   F   ?
7. The robber succeeded in getting the woman's money before
   he left.   T   F   ?
8. There was no robber.   T   F   ?
9. Students notified the police.   T   F   ?
10. This is a story about a woman, her husband, and some stu-
    dents.   T   F   ?

These are the answers you should have marked, with some indication of the reasons for the correct answers.

1. ? The woman could have been principal, the janitor, or a visiting parent.
2. ? Lights are on in classrooms both during the day and the night, so we can't say for certain.
3. ? The person who demanded the money was a man. We do not know for sure that he was a robber. For example, the woman and her husband might have had a fight that morning. She might have forgotten to give him the check book or the keys to the house, and he has come to get them. His abruptness reveals his anger.
4. ? We assume that students are young, but this could be an adult education class. Hence, the man who demanded money could have been one of the students.
5. T This was confirmed by the story.
6. ? We assume that this is false, based on the assumption that this is the bell that assembles the students at the beginning of the day, after lunch, or between classes. It is possible, however, that during a fire drill some students would pass through another classroom on their way out of the building. This classroom might be on their exit path.
7. ? First, we don't know if there was a robber. Second, we don't know what he took from her purse or even if he got what he wanted since that part of the story states, "After the purse was emptied, the man left abruptly."
8. ? Probably false, but the man could be someone else, as explained in #3.
9. F The woman notified the police.
10. ? We don't assume so, but it could be (see #3 again).

This exercise is intended to be tricky and amusing, but it also serves to demonstrate the extent to which many of us treat our inferences as facts.

NOTES

1. *The American Heritage Dictionary of the English Language,* New College Edition (Boston: Houghton Mifflin Company, 1979), p. 469.
2. From a handout obtained at a management training workshop (source unknown).
3. *Ibid.*
4. *Ibid.*
5. *American Heritage,* p. 1264.
6. Norman Cousins, "The Environment of Language," *Saturday Review* (April 1967), p. 36.
7. *Ibid.*

chapter *3*

The Audience as Listeners

CHAPTER OBJECTIVE

After studying this chapter you should be able to:

1. Explain the importance of listening.
2. List and describe common problems associated with listening.
3. List guidelines for effective listening.
4. Devise and implement your own strategy for improved listening.

INTRODUCTION

Throughout our lives we are evaluated on the basis of how well we listen. The first grader's report card assesses the extent to which he or she is attentive, follows orders, and listens when others are talking. As teenagers, our parents accuse us of daydreaming rather than listening; similarly, we believe that they do not really listen to our emerging and often controversial views. Later, in secondary schools and in college, we spend endless hours listening to teachers and professors drone on and on. In many instances, how well we listen will determine our final grade.

The significance of listening increases when we enter the world of work as adults. Studies show that we typically spend about 70 percent of every day in some form of verbal communication. Of that time, 9 percent is spent in writing, 16 percent in reading, 30 percent in talking, and 45 percent in listening (1). Most managers spend many hours talking on the telephone, being briefed, listening to proposal presentations, and hearing others' views in decision-making groups. Moreover, even nonmanagement personnel spend many hours of every work day listening to problems, complaints, ideas, and information. In a sense, then, their employers are actually paying them to listen. Listening is a valuable activity!

When we listen effectively, we increase the chances of experiencing certain positive outcomes. *First, we can obtain a good deal of information.* It has been estimated, for example, that nearly 60 percent of our ideas come from some medium other than print. That is, we learn from listening to the radio and television and from listening to other people talk (2). Equally important, good listeners usually have better interpersonal relationships. *Listening to someone is an excellent way to show that we care.* And listening is usually reciprocated. *We also gain a clearer sense of who we are and what we value through listening.* Listening allows us to compare and contrast ourselves with others so as to gain a sense of personal identity. *Finally, those who know how to listen are often better speakers.* By observing the way others communicate, we can gain some understanding of what they find tasteful, sound, strategic, and interesting. And, of course, one of the best ways to analyze an audience is to listen to what they say about themselves as you interact with them before or after your speech.

In spite of the importance of listening, most of us are terribly inefficient listeners. Right after a public speech we typically recall only about half of what was said, and within a few months our recall is reduced to only 25 percent. Some contend that ineffective listening is a chief cause of communication failure in the business world (3). Why do we listen so poorly? What can be done about it? For you, as a beginning public speaker, these questions are especially important. Not only do you need good listening skills for the reasons we have discussed above, but when you actually speak in public you will be confronted with a listening audience.

To be effective as a public speaker you must examine your audience so that you can learn something about their needs, values, and ways of thinking. But first it is crucial that you understand your audience *as listeners.* Quite apart from an audience's particular demographic characteristics—whether they are largely male or female, under 30 or over 60, high school dropouts or M.B.A.s from Harvard, wealthy or on welfare—they are all listeners. If you are to be successful in communicating with them, you need to be knowledgeable about the listening process. In particular, you should be able to identify common listening problems which, if understood and anticipated, can be minimized, managed, or possibly completely avoided.

THE TROUBLES WITH LISTENING

The Passivity Syndrome

The average listener is unfamiliar with statistics on inefficient listening. Even if he or she could be introduced to such information, it is unlikely that the resulting impact would be great. Why? First, most of us like to believe that we are exceptional. Since statistics on poor listening are based on sampling and inference, we can readily assume that they don't apply to us. Besides, essentially we believe that listening is easy. We've been doing it for years and for many hours during every day, especially as students; hence, we are well rehearsed. Moreover, many of us feel that our primary responsibility as listening audience members is to make sure that our bodies are in the seats at the appointed hour. From that point on, we believe, it is up to the speaker to make us want to listen: if he fails, how unfortunate for him!

The line of reasoning described in the preceding paragraph represents the *passivity syndrome.* It is rooted in a liner and very traditional view of communication which assumes that the speaker acts and the listener reacts, that the speaker controls and the listener is controlled. The listener who thinks this way probably doesn't mind "relinquishing his responsibility" for the outcome of the communication transactions. He might, however, be less enchanted with the notion of losing control, being dominated, or responding with passivity and compliance. Yet, these are all logical extensions of the passivity syndrome.

The audience member who wants to be an effective listener must begin by recognizing that listening is an *active process.* Anyone can make us hear simply by turning up the volume. But no one can make us listen. *We have to want to listen and we have to be willing to work at it.* Hopefully, the speaker will encourage us by presenting his ideas in an interesting, well-supported, organized, and effectively delivered manner. But if he doesn't, if he is disorganized, speaks in a monotone, and plays with his pen that doesn't let us off the hook. After all, most speakers have some weaknesses and, frankly, need our cooperation and assistance. Moreover, our attendance at a public speaking event represents a significant investment of valuable time. If we attend a public lecture because we hope to learn, to grow, to be stimulated, or to discover action strategies and we come away empty handed, surely we must recognize that wherever the "fault" may lie, the *outcome* is our problem. *Thus, we should strive to listen effectively for the sake of ourselves as well as the speaker.*

The Environment that Overwhelms

Independence is a traditional American value. Usually we admire individuals who are in charge of themselves, are able to behave with reasonable consistency, and do not allow themselves to be governed by their surroundings. As audience members, however, we often behave as if we can listen effectively only when the environment permits us to do so. We become extremely sensitive to distractions in our surroundings, using them as easy excuses for our inability to listen. We complain, for example, that the room is too hot or too cold, too large or too crowded, has poor acoustics, or is open to outside noise. We sit in the last row and complain that the speaker's voice doesn't carry well. In class we plant ourselves next to two talkative fraternity brothers and we learn a great deal about Sigma Chi but almost nothing about calculus. We sit by an open window and then find ourselves distracted by a lawnmower, the shouts of children, or the beauty of the view. Clearly we are good at this blame-placing game. We tell ourselves that we had every good intention of listening, but we were simply overwhelmed by environmental distractions.

There are times, of course, when speeches are made in rooms that are poorly ventilated, crowded, or noisy. Distractions are often real, as well as imagined.

A student listens intently to his teacher in order to learn. Students acquire knowledge that they can use by listening actively. (Photo courtesy of Peter Southwick, Stock, Boston.)

Yet, the fact that a listening situation is less than ideal does not mean that we are free to relax and daydream. In most instances we can overcome environmental disturbances if we so desire. Think of a time when you really wanted to talk to someone, but for one reason or another the circumstances were difficult. For example, you get a phone call from an old friend from high school who happens to be stationed with the Air Force in Germany. You haven't spoken with him for several years and although the connection is filled with cracks, squeaks, and remote but interfering voices, you strain your ears and you listen. Because you want to hear what he has to say, you are able to overcome annoying distractions. Similarly, in most public communication settings we are capable of receiving the intended message if we are motivated to listen, regardless of situational irritations.

Eyes Are Not for Listening

Everyone is aware of the power of first impressions. When we first meet a person we instantly begin the process of evaluation. Although we may doubt the reasoned worth of snap judgments, we make them with regularity. Sometimes the initial impression is quickly counteracted by subsequent events. On other occasions early impressions have a more enduring impact. We know, for example, that employers rarely change their judgments of job applicants after the first five minutes, although the typical interview lasts for thirty minutes (4). One major component of the first impression is the individual's physical appearance. In fact, in the absence of additional information, appearance may be the sole basis for early judgments.

The public speaking situation presents a special problem in this regard in that most public speakers are "on display" before they make their speeches. Seated at a luncheon table or on a speaker's platform they can be viewed but are not yet permitted to address the audience. Hence, there is plenty of time for listeners to look at them and form early, and often stereotypic, impressions about their basic nature and quality. We may decide, for example, that a speaker is a "woman's-libber" because she is braless, or "masculine" because she is wearing a skirted suit. Also in trouble is the man whose trousers are too short or whose hair is too long. We base our judgments on such details as hair style, makeup, clothing, and jewelry, as well as on body build and facial attractiveness. Thus, long before the speaker opens her mouth, we have recorded an impression.

However, we should not use the initial impression as the basis for early judgment. We must not allow ourselves to perceive selectively so that we only hear what will reinforce the first impression. If we do, we have judged the speaker as if she were a contestant in a beauty pageant or a dress review. It is true, of course, that nonverbal communication is important and cannot be ignored, but what we observe with the eyes is only a beginning. We are there to listen to the speaker's complete presentation. Then, on the basis of what we have heard and observed, we are better able to make some reasoned evaluation.

Fixating on Delivery

Most speech teachers and theorists agree that delivery is an important component of effective public speaking. But it is only one component. Among listeners, however, there is a tendency to focus on the speaker's delivery as if it were the only element of the speech worthy of note. When asked to comment on a fellow class member's speech, college students typically say, "He had a really nice voice," "I liked the way she used her hands," or "I wish he hadn't paced back and forth so much." Delivery is important and cannot be overlooked, but as listeners we must take great pains lest we leave a public communication event with a concise critique of the speaker's delivery and only a vague recollection of the speaker's ideas.

Rarely do we attend public speeches so that we can criticize delivery. Our goals are usually related to some desire to expand our knowledge, gain interesting insights, or hear insightful arguments on behalf of an important cause. But judgments about delivery by themselves are fairly empty accomplishments. *Delivery is, after all, method rather than substance.* As method it is important in that it reinforces, elaborates, accents, or contradicts the speaker's message. It would be legitimate, for example, to note that the speaker's arguments seemed weak with rather sparse supporting evidence. You might further observe that the speaker's delivery was monotonous, with poor eye contact and no bodily movement or gestures. Together these observations might lead you to conclude that the speaker didn't seem very excited about his own ideas. Hence, your judgment, based jointly on content and delivery, is legitimately negative. Standing alone, however, delivery is a relatively superficial component of public communication and should not be used as the sole or even the major determinant of listener response.

Mental Games

Most of us are quite comfortable when we perceive our world to be in a state of balance. We enjoy chatting with people who seem similar to ourselves and normally we prefer public speakers whose basic thinking is in line with our own. This desire for harmony, consistency, and balance may not be conscious, but it can cause us to react defensively whenever we are exposed to ideas that challenge our world view. If the issue under discussion is relatively insignificant to us, we may take it in stride. When a public speaker questions our thinking on some matter central to our value system, however, we may be jarred into defensiveness. Depending upon your value system, you might become quite distressed when hearing a speaker threaten your financial security, self-esteem, or sense of morality. During the presidential debates of 1980, for example, Ronald Reagan remarked that he might reinstate the GI Bill. Many audience members reacted adversely, pondering over where the money for this program might come from and whether they would be called upon to contribute. Others were distressed over positions taken by Reagan or Carter or both on women's rights, national defense, the economy, and abortion. In response to their disagreement, they turned off the television, started reading the newspaper, or began talking among themselves.

In a regular public speaking situation the listener does not have so many retaliatory options at her disposal. Even so, it is always possible to turn the speaker off mentally. We may do this either by pretending to listen while turning our minds to other affairs or by engaging in mental rebuttal. Either technique represents a listening hazard. With the former, we feign attentiveness (and we are very good at that!) while allowing ourselves to fantasize, plan the evening ahead, or reflect upon our day. Not only is this (pretending to listen) an act of dishonesty, but it is a waste of time.

The second tactic, mental argument, is somewhat preferable in that we do remain actively involved in thinking about the speech topic. But it has nothing to do with listening to the speaker. In fact, as we carefully refute the speaker's statistics, philosophical foundation, or analytical techniques, we actually engage ourselves in a kind of dialogue. While listening to ourselves, we tune out the speaker. After the speech is finished we know what the speaker said up to a point, but the remainder of the speech escaped us. It is hardly surprising, then, that during question and answer periods listeners often ask for information that the speaker has already provided. Hence, part of the questioning period is wasted by needless reiteration of points already discussed and the listener is embarrassed when the speaker points out that she has already provided the requested information.

As effective listeners we must allow the speaker to state her complete case. It is perfectly acceptable to recognize disagreement during the speech, but you should simply make note of it, put it aside, and listen to the rest of the argument. *After having listened to a complete statement of the speaker's point of view, you are then equipped to react intelligently and justly to points raised along the way.*

Words that Provoke

Our language is powerful. Not only does language create social reality, as we pointed out in Chapter 2, but it often elicits strong reactions from those who listen to it. Most well-educated women, for example, are keenly aware of sexism in our language and respond adversely whenever a speaker consistently uses male pronouns to refer to both genders. Moreover, many of our most commonly used words are rich with associative or connotative meaning; that is, they are rich with feelings, emotions, and experiential value. Intelligent speakers understand the power of language and strive to use it to enhance their arguments. A speaker might associate her cause, for example, with freedom, democracy, independence of thought, and self-respect, all of which are highly valued by Americans. A different strategy might be to define those opposed to her as warmongers, communists, fools, or thieves. In either case the speaker is hoping that the listeners' reactions to these highly evaluative words will affect their judgments of the concepts or individuals she is discussing.

Every society has "god" and "devil" terms, words to which most of us respond very strongly and in an extremely polarized fashion. When, as listeners, we hear these highly provocative words and phrases, we run the risk of becoming so overpowered by the feelings, experiences, and attitudes the words bring to mind that we fail to examine the accompanying idea. The speaker says, "Only a godless society could condone abortion. Those who advocate abortion stand as advocates of murder." Unless the listener is very careful, she may find herself opposed to abortion because she is strongly opposed to the idea of being a "godless murderer." To better determine her position, however, she needs to examine the argument being advanced so that she might judge its logical merit.

Public speakers vary in their sensitivity to language and in their desire or ability to use the language in an emotionally provocative manner. It is not unethical to choose words rich with associative meaning, unless one's purpose is to prevent the listener from thinking rationally about the subject. Even so, as listeners we must recognize that we can be lulled into a false sense of harmony by pretty words or we may allow ourselves to be filled with rage, dismay, or revulsion because of ugly words. *The careful listener looks for ideas embedded in the speech so that later she can decide whether she accepts or rejects them.*

Note-Taking Hazards

Most of us have less than perfect memories. Even if we are striving to listen carefully and conscientiously, we will still have some problems with accurate and complete recall. In dealing with this problem, most of us turn to some form of note-taking to provide a more accurate record of what the speaker said. In general, note-taking is a laudable listening aid. Because it requires some action on our part, we are reminded that good listening is an active process. It is impossible to remain completely passive while taking notes. In addition, note-taking takes time. Since we can think so much more rapidly than the speaker can talk, taking notes can help us synchronize our tempo with the speaker's. (In fact, we may find ourselves wishing he'd slow down or repeat himself!) Finally, and most obviously, note-taking helps us to remember. Based on our notes, we might then ask questions after the speech and take home with us some recorded information to ponder and possibly use in the future.

Note-taking is no more than a technique, which like other techniques, can be used adeptly or improperly. Perhaps the most significant note-taking hazard is not knowing what to write down. Listeners tend to err in writing down either too little or too much. Jotting down only an occasional word or phrase is probably not adequate to remind you later of the point the speaker made. Neither, however, do you need a virtual transcript of the speaker's remarks. In fact, unless you know shorthand or are planning to bring a tape recorder, it is almost impossible to keep a complete running account of the speaker's message. What you need, then, is a compromise, in which you record major ideas with occasional words or phrases to remind you of particularly striking or controversial examples or other evidence. You should end up with a basic outline of the speech, similar to the one being used by the speaker. In Chapter 8 you will find a sample outline to illustrate one form a good outline might take.

GUIDELINES FOR EFFECTIVE LISTENING

Implicit in our discussion of listening problems are some suggestions about how you might become a more effective listener. In this final section of the chapter I will synthesize these into a checklist of guidelines for effective listening behavior. The next time you plan to attend a public communication event, consult this list. After it is over, re-examine the list to determine your success and to discover what does or does not work for you. Whether you are speaking or listening, you will need to make personal adjustments in any set of general guidelines. The following, then, represents guiding principles rather than absolute rules.

1. *Prepare yourself for listening.* Arrive on time. Find a seat where you can hear and see. Bring note-taking materials. Think openmindedly about the subject. Think about the chance to learn and grow and hear some interesting arguments. Prepare to be involved actively in the communication event.

2. *Listen for a central theme.* Most speeches possess some unity; that is, there is a major theme to which all of the supporting elements relate (or should relate). Try to identify the speech's major theme fairly early in the speech. Some speakers will tell you directly: for example, "I am here today to convince you of the need for a new library in this community." Once you have discovered the speech's basic theme, write it down.

3. *Listen for major points.* The speaker's basic arguments or lines of thought should relate to the major theme in a way that reveals some sense of unity or overall pattern. Look for the major arguments and write them down, mentally noting how they relate to the major thrust of the speech. The speaker might, for example, establish her new library theme by pointing out that: (a) the old library no longer meets federal and state fire regulation standards, (b) the old library is too small to accommodate

the number of patrons who presently seek its use, (c) it is impossible to renovate the old library due to structural deficiencies, and (d) a new library is affordable and offers numerous advantages to the community. As you are able to detect the major arguments, the speech's outline begins to emerge.

4. *Listen for evidence.* Good public speakers will do more than make assertions; they will also support their views with evidence. Later you will study criteria for the examination of evidence. Now you need to recognize, however, that the quality of an argument is largely determined by its development. How is it important? Who says, for example, that the old library doesn't meet fire regulations? What are those regulations? What are the specific ways in which the library violates those rules? Can/should the laws be revised? In responding to these kinds of questions, the speaker should use statistics, testimony, examples, and illustrations. As a good listener, you must notice the kind and quality of support the speaker introduces.

5. *Listen for reasoning.* Public speakers do not simply present evidence; they also draw conclusions from the evidence. Later in this book you will study reasoning processes. You might recognize now, however, that conclusions drawn from evidence can be either sound or unsound. A good listener is alert to the possibility of errors in reasoning and carefully examines the soundness of the speaker's conclusions.

6. *Listen to the complete speech.* It is one thing to suspend your judgment at the beginning of the speech, but it is quite another to maintain your open-mindedness until the speaker is finished. This is perhaps the most difficult part of the listening process because it requires a sustained commitment to active and objective listening. When you detect a piece of poor evidence or unsound reasoning, it is difficult not to make some hasty judgment about the speaker's competence. But you cannot make a just assessment of any speaker's remarks until you have heard them all.

7. *When the speech is over, weigh, consider, and evaluate the speaker's remarks.* Listeners have every right to interpret and evaluate any speaker's ideas. That judgment appropriately comes at the end of the speech. Our evaluations should center on such matters as organization, content, and delivery.

The following is a speaker evaluation form, which suggests concrete criteria you might find helpful in judging the quality of a speech.

SPEAKER EVALUATION FORM

The ratings to be used in the following form should be interpreted thus: SA = Strongly Agree, A = Agree, N = Neutral or Not applicable, D = Disagree, and SD = Strongly Disagree.

1. The speech had a clearly stated purpose.   SA A N D SD
2. The speaker used an attention-arousing introduction.   SA A N D SD

3. The topic was sufficiently narrow, given the time constraints. SA A N D SD

4. The speaker attempted to adapt his or her topic to the needs and interests of the audience. SA A N D SD

5. The speech was well organized in terms of unity, coherence, conciseness, relevance, and comprehensiveness. SA A N D SD

6. The speaker seemed highly credible as a source of information on this topic. SA A N D SD

7. The speaker's ideas were well supported with facts, statistics, illustrations, examples, comparisons, or other appropriate devices. SA A N D SD

8. The speaker used a variety of different sources. SA A N D SD

9. The speaker's sources were very reputable. SA A N D SD

10. The speaker's analysis of the problem seemed sound. SA A N D SD

11. The speaker made appropriate reference to his or her sources of information. SA A N D SD

12. The solution advocated by the speaker seemed valid, useful, manageable, and/or appropriate. SA A N D SD

13. The speaker made effective eye contact. SA A N D SD

14. The speaker seemed involved in his or her speech. SA A N D SD

15. The speaker used appropriate gestures and/or bodily movement. SA A N D SD

16. The speaker projected his or her voice adequately. SA A N D SD

17. The speaker used his or her notes skillfully. SA A N D SD

18. The speaker's visual aids enhanced the clarity and interest of the presentation. SA A N D SD

19. The speaker's conclusion had substantial impact. SA A N D SD

20. The speaker responded intelligently to questions. SA A N D SD

Please comment in any aspect of the speaker's content, organization, or delivery that you found particularly good or in need of improvement:

Concluding Notes

As you prepare to read the remainder of this book, you should refer to this chapter with regularity. Among the people who gather to hear you speak, you will find abundant examples of the listening problems I have identified above. Your audience members will gaze, doze, mentally retaliate, and examine the length of your hair. They will assume that the burden of proof is upon you to interest them, entertain them, and make them want to listen. Not all listeners, but enough, will possess such poor habits, and if these matters are not acknowledged and managed, they could greatly reduce your impact as a public speaker. If, for example, you do not practice your speech and your delivery is sloppy, you may fall prey to those who fixate on delivery. If you do not concern yourself with your appearance, those who listen with their eyes may never hear a word you utter. And if you are dull, you may lose them all!

There will also be, however, individuals in your audiences who have studied listening and who understand what to look for and how to examine your speech justly. These persons will be listening for your central theme, your supporting arguments, the quality of your evidence, and the soundness of your reasoning. It is vital, therefore, that you learn to manage these communication variables effectively.

EXERCISES

1. Most of us have listening problems in interpersonal as well as in public communication settings. To gain some insights into your own listening skills, ask another person to sit with you for a few minutes and discuss some subject of mutual concern. If possible, choose a subject about which you do not completely agree. Then observe the following rule: No one may talk until he or she has paraphrased (repeated the thrust of) the remarks of the other person to his or her satisfaction. Your conversation should proceed something like this:

    Bob: States a point of view, with or without elaboration.
    Pat: Describes his understanding of Bob's comments.
    Bob: Agrees or disagrees with Pat's paraphrase, corrects him if necessary. (Pat may have to try the paraphrase again if he was initially far off base and once again seek Bob's confirmation.)
    Pat: Agrees or disagrees with Bob's paraphrase, etc.

   This dialogue can continue until you are ready to stop. Each of you may take notes if you desire.
   When you are finished, discuss your listening problems. What was most difficult to listen to? Did your emotions ever get in the way? Were there words you reacted strongly to? Any physical distractions? What was the major thrust of the other person's point of view? How might you improve as a listener?
2. Choose a public speaking event to attend. You might choose a sermon, political speech, informative speech, or technical report. Go a few minutes early. Observe the *listening environment.* Make a list of everything you see, hear, or feel which might serve as a listening distraction. For example, you might note a crowded room, open windows, noisy air conditioner, door opening out onto a busy hallway, poor acoustics, a sensitive microphone, etc. Now spend a few minutes observing other *audience members.* What are they doing? Have they seated themselves comfortably? Are they taking notes, doodling? Do they appear attentive? How do you know? Make a list of problems you observe. Finally, look at the *speaker.* Does he or she possess any characteristics that

might prove distracting? For example, he or she might be dressed strangely, have a harsh voice, or gesture dramatically. Of course, problems vary as we move from one listening context to another, but many listening hazards are recurrent or represent variations of the same basic problem.

3. Now choose another public communication event. Armed with your own list of listening hazards and the information about listening provided in this book, fill out the form that follows.

Speaker: _____ Date: _____

Topic: _____

Occasion: _____

1. Identify the speaker's central theme/purpose.

2. Make an outline of the major points of the speech. Major ideas should go under Roman numerals I, II, and III, with supporting points under A, B, C, and D.

I.
  A.
  B.
  C.
  D.

II.
  A.
  B.
  C.
  D.

  A.
  B.
  C.
  D.

3. How easily could you follow the speaker's pattern of organization?

4. What strengths and weaknesses in evidence and reasoning did you detect?

5. How did the speaker's delivery aid or hinder the effective communication of his or her message?

6. What are your questions/comments?

NOTES

1. Ralph C. Nichols and Leonard A. Stevens, *Are Your Listening?* (New York: McGraw-Hill, 1957).
2. William Norwood Brigance, *Speech: Its Techniques and Disciplines in a Free Society* (New York: Appleton-Century-Crofts, 1961).
3. M. Applegate, "Are You a Good Listener?" *Western Business and Industry* (Feb. 1965), pp. 26–27.
4. Mary Bakeman et al., *Job Seeking Skills Reference Manual,* 3rd ed. (Minneapolis: Minnesota Rehabilitation Center, Inc., 1971), p. 57.

chapter 4

Speech Anxiety

CHAPTER OBJECTIVES

After studying this chapter you should be able to:

1. Describe the nature of speech anxiety.
2. List the causes of speech anxiety.
3. Disprove speech fright misconceptions.
4. Devise and implement a strategy for handling your own speech anxiety.

INTRODUCTION

Few of us approach a chance to make a speech with sheer enthusiasm. Even if we have something we really want to say, if we feel honored to have been asked to talk, or if we have volunteered to speak, as the day of the speech draws near we begin to experience some apprehension: Have I prepared adequately? Will the audience like me? Will my mind go blank when I start to talk? These are only a few of the questions that whirl through our minds and cause our stomachs to churn. Perhaps we find ourselves thinking, "Maybe I could get sick (or die) on the day of the speech."

Whether you call it speech anxiety or stage fright or communication apprehension (1) you need to know about it for several reasons. First, if it is unanticipated and poorly understood, speech anxiety can be extremely debilitating to you as a public speaker. You could have a bad communication experience which might have been avoided. Second, there are many misconceptions about speech anxiety which, if left unclarified, serve to intensify the apprehension you experience. Finally, strategies exist for dealing with speech anxiety which, if known and practiced, can help reduce your anxiety and allow your speechmaking to be not just a bearable but an enjoyable communication experience as well.

WHAT IS SPEECH ANXIETY?

Nearly all of us love attention. As children we liked it when our parents paid attention to us. Now, when a friend asks for our input on a pressing personal decision and listens carefully to our ideas, we feel good. Likewise, we enjoy having our siblings, peers, and instructors give us their undivided attention. It makes us feel important. We can scarcely get enough of it. Strangely enough, however, when a roomful of people turn their eyes upon us as we are about to make a speech, we become afraid. One might conclude that attention is beneficial only when it comes in small doses.

The fear, the timidity, the apprehension we experience when we speak in front of others is speech anxiety. Of course, we may feel apprehensive about almost any kind of communication encounter. If, for example, you have ever prepared to talk with a longtime flame who you think is about to tell you that she wants to date someone else, if your professor has called you in to her office to discuss your poor attendance record, or if a police officer has motioned you to the side of the highway for "an interview," you know what communication apprehension is all about. We are, however, far more likely to be apprehensive about speaking in front of an audience of strangers than with those we know well in interpersonal and small group settings.

Causes of Speech Anxiety

Since speakers are individuals, different factors in public communication events will generate anxiety for each of them. Some speakers bring their fears with them, perhaps in the form of a poorly prepared speech. Others become anxious upon seeing the audience for the first time. Still others experience fear when they notice during the early moments of the speech that their hands are shaking. However, there are several causes of speech anxiety that affect almost all of us.

Perhaps the single most potent cause of speech anxiety is the knowledge that we are being evaluated. We dislike the idea of being judged in most any human communication context. In fact, many contemporary psychologists contend that we cannot have effective interpersonal relationships in a context of judgment (2). Not only does evaluation occur whenever we make a speech, but the judgment is largely one-way, that is, the audience "rates" the speaker. Rarely does one hear a speaker muttering as he leaves the platform, "Good grief, what a lousy audience! I'll never grace them with my presence again!" It is not uncommon, however, to hear listeners whisper to each other, "I thought she'd have something interesting to say. I'm really disappointed," or "I can't believe how disorganized he is. He must have written his speech on the airplane." Because of this type of judgmental response, *evaluation apprehension* is a major cause of speech anxiety.

Beside the evaluative function that most audiences play, there are other *audience characteristics* that may contribute to our sense of insecurity. If, for example, we are speaking to a group of people of high *status,* we may feel uncomfortable. This is especially the case if the audience's status is higher than our own and we are all part of the same group or organization. Suppose that you have been asked to speak to the Board of Trustees at the university you attend. Having experienced the frustration of trying to park your car on campus, you decided to investigate available parking facilities at comparable schools. As part of your speech class you needed a campus-related problem to research. From your research you developed a proposal for changing the parking arrangements at your own institution, including a different fee structure, a new parking garage limited to students, and enhanced facilities for the handicapped. Your proposal so impressed your speech instructor that he mentioned your ideas to the dean, who brought the matter to the attention of the vice president. The vice president then asked you to represent the student body by presenting your plan to the Board. In this situation you are not only speaking to people who will evaluate your ideas and decide whether to support them but you are also speaking to people you would like to impress. They are important in your view, and they might even have some influence over your own academic future. Clearly, status perceptions have substantial impact on speech anxiety.

Another audience characteristic of potential significance is *size.* Most speakers prefer small- or medium-sized audiences. With huge audiences it is easy to get the feeling that if we flop, we flop more significantly since so many people know about it. Whatever judgment is being made is also magnified because instead of having two dozen listeners remark that you were dull, you have 200, which makes the judgment seem more binding. Dealing with large audiences is also difficult in that it is almost impossible to feel that you are speaking directly to any one among them. You may even find yourself on a stage in a blackened auditorium with spotlights blinding you so that the audience is something you can only hear from time to time but cannot see. Of course, not all speakers respond identically to audience size. Some actually feel safer with large audiences because the communication situation can remain impersonal, and they are more comfortable maintaining considerable distance from the audience, both physically and psychologically. This is not as common, however, as the preference for smaller audiences.

Another relevant audience characteristic is *familiarity.* Most of us prefer talking with people we know than with a group of strangers. Actually, the public speaking situation is unusual in that not only are we in the position of having to talk at length to complete strangers (something our mothers taught us never to do!), but these strangers are staring at us for an extended period of time. When we must speak in front of an unfamiliar audience, it is easy to become anxious because they are learning a great deal about us and our ideas while we know relatively little about them. It is important to gather information about the audience before making the speech in order to feel more relaxed about the response they are likely to make. As with the size factor, not all speakers take the same position. Some prefer to deal with strangers. When they must speak in

A young person may feel nervous while addressing an older, more experienced group of people. The composition of an audience does influence the anxiety that a speaker may feel. (Photo courtesy of Owen Frank, Stock, Boston.)

front of those they know and love, they feel great pressure to "come through" and not disappoint anyone. Whatever your personal stand on this issue, audience familiarity is likely to be a factor affecting your feelings of security.

A final pertinent audience variable is *perceived similarity*. If you believe that the audience's position is similar to your own, that they essentially agree with you, you will most likely experience less speech fright than if you believe them to be opposed to your views. Also important here are your perceptions of the audience's feelings toward you as a person. Suppose you must speak to a group of people who hold you in high personal regard, but you know that your position differs from theirs. This situation is far more palatable than one in which you believe you lack credibility and are planning to advocate an unpopular point of view. In the latter instance speaker anxiety may be severe.

Clearly audience variables can create a full measure of speech fright. Similarly, public speakers may bring with them certain potential sources of speech anxiety. Suppose, for example, that you are a perfectionist. You have high expectations for your own behavior and constantly demand much of yourself. Now you rise to make a speech. You introduce the speech with a humorous story and the audience remains politely silent. Or you get your tongue twisted. Or you leave out a point and have to go back to it. The list could go on and on. How do you feel? As a perfectionist you would probably condemn yourself as a complete failure. Obviously, *self-expectations* are vital. If they are unreasonably high, they may produce great anxiety. *No public speaker is perfect. If you demand perfection of yourself, you will usually be disappointed.* And more importantly you will most likely experience greater tension before you make the speech. High expectations for one's own behavior are commendable. Such expectations, however, should leave room for one's humanity.

The public speaker may also experience considerable anxiety because of his or her own speech. *If the speaker has prepared poorly, if the speech is disorganized, poorly documented, or lacking in interest, the speaker may have real cause for fear.* As one sits quietly moments before the speech, it is difficult to be dishonest with oneself. If you, as the speaker, are afraid you will lose your place because you have never practiced with your notes, if you think the audience will find you dull because you yourself find the speech dull, or if you fear someone will ask you for more information after the speech and you don't have any more information, you are likely to feel a sense of impending doom. In contrast, when you know that you have prepared thoroughly, your speech anxiety should be far more manageable.

Finally, some speakers have problems with speech fright simply because they do not understand the physiological reactions which often accompany it. We turn now to an examination of those reactions.

The Physiology of Speech Anxiety

Speech anxiety is a fear response. Your body reacts to your fear as it would in any fear-producing situation. If you were hurrying down a dark avenue on your way home from work one night and you became aware of quickening footsteps behind you, changes would begin to take place within your body. Your heart would beat rapidly and your blood pressure would rise (the results of increases in adrenalin and thyroxin). The pupils of your eyes would dilate. Increased sugar in your blood would give you more than your normal level of energy. If you had food in your stomach, your body would cease to digest it. You would breathe more rapidly and less deeply. Even the hairs on your arms and legs would stand on end! Quite probably you would take flight as a response to this fear-producing situation.

Your bodily responses to speech anxiety are similar to those described above. You may feel a great desire to flee or at the very least to get the speech over with quickly so that you can go home and recover! Although general bodily reaction patterns are much alike, there will also be considerable variation among individuals. Examine the list of Anxiety Outcomes in Table 4.1. They represent physiological effects that people often experience before or while giving a speech.

The list is scarcely comprehensive. Speech anxiety can generate many reactions. If you have experienced some or many of them, you have probably learned to recognize them as "dread symptoms." When you feel them coming on, you

Table 4.1   ANXIETY OUTCOMES

_____   Parched mouth

_____   Butterflies in the stomach

_____   Frog in the throat

_____   Shortness of breath

_____   Too much saliva

_____   Nausea

_____   Shaking voice

_____   Trembling legs (or hands)

_____   Clammy hands

_____   Icy hands

_____   Loss of memory

_____   Frozen facial expression

_____   Flushed cheeks

_____   Red throat blotches

_____   Nervous pacing

_____   Clinging to the podium

_____   Darting eyes (looking everywhere but at the audience)

_____   Hot flashes

_____   Feeling weak all over

_____   Tingling spine

_____   Sudden need to visit the bathroom

_____   Inability to gesture

_____   The "you know" syndrome (also included are "um," "uh," and "well")

_____   Giggling when nothing is funny

may feel even more apprehensive. In turn, this apprehension generates still more nervous energy, which only aggravates and enhances the fear reactions you are already experiencing. Hence, the process is cyclical, as depicted in Figure 4.1. We respond adversely to our recognition of the body's responses to speech anxiety, in part, because we labor under several misconceptions.

MISCONCEPTIONS ABOUT SPEECH ANXIETY

Everyone Will Know

If you ever did anything really naughty when you were a child (like letting your pet fish swim in the toilet bowl for a few minutes), you probably remember feeling that as soon as your parents saw you they would know that you had been up to no good. Even if all the evidence had been removed (the fish was safely back in its own bowl), you still felt that you would get caught; you believed that your parents could read your mind. Similarly, as public speakers we often act as if we believe that the audience knows exactly what we are feeling. They can hear our

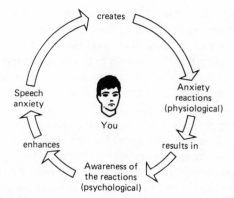

Figure 4.1

throbbing hearts, see our quivering limbs, and feel our sweaty palms. Rest assured: audiences are rarely aware of speaker anxiety. Even if they recognize that a speaker is nervous, chances are they will grossly underestimate the intensity of her speech fright. Even some trained speech teachers have difficulty judging the amount of nervousness being experienced by their students (3). In fact, most listeners rate speakers as significantly less anxious than the speakers rate themselves. Apparently most of us are pretty good at putting up an effective façade. We are capable of projecting an aura of confidence and calmness, even in the midst of considerable inner turmoil.

Of course, whether or not the audience is aware of a speaker's nervousness will depend in part upon environmental factors. If you are speaking to hundreds of people in an auditorium, there will be so much distance between you and even the closest audience member that judging your anxiety responses will be virtually impossible. In fact, any time you speak from behind a podium, you have some "protection" from audience scrutiny. If your knees are knocking, no one will ever know. Of course, you cannot always count on having a podium, and you certainly will speak to audiences of various sizes in both formal/distant and close/intimate situations. Sometimes you will find yourself only a few feet from the audience. When such is the case, you are more vulnerable to audience scrutiny. *That's why it is important to know how to manage your speech anxiety as well as understand it.*

Speech Anxiety Will Intensify as the Speech Goes On

One of the advantages of making a public speech is that you have a chance to make a statement about a subject you believe to be significant. Although you may feel quite anxious before and during the early moments of your speech, as you continue to discuss your topic you may find yourself getting excited about what you are saying. As you begin to focus more on your message and the people to whom you are speaking, your speech anxiety will often diminish significantly rather than intensify. After all, as you continue to talk you are noting certain things: you are not passing out, the audience *does* seem interested (or at least they are sticking with you), and you *do* care about what you are saying. Probably you have noticed the emphasis I have placed on your concern for the speech topic. Sometimes speakers settle on any old topic because they are rushed and have to commit themselves early on or because they feel required to speak. (College students are particularly susceptible to this latter problem since their speeches are often class assignments.) Later these speakers may react to their speechmaking as a simple academic exercise. They have little to notice beside their nervousness since they have minimal concern for their subject.

You may wonder why a speaker with such a frivolous attitude would even encounter speech anxiety. After all, why should we be afraid of something that doesn't matter to us? Speech anxiety occurs in these instances because we are still aware of our personal responsibility for the speech. We selected the topic, we committed ourselves to the position we are about to take, and we will be judged. Moreover, when we know that we haven't planned the speech as we should, either through poor topic selection or inadequate research or practice, we tend to feel guilty: we haven't done our homework, so we deserve to "fail." These kinds of thoughts are far from reassuring. In fact, when poorly prepared, we have every right to be worried. Under those conditions we are quite likely to hem and haw, forget the point we were making, ramble, and stammer. That's enough to make anyone nervous!

In contrast, the public speaker who is well prepared and who is speaking about a topic of great concern to both him and the audience can legitimately say to himself when the first anxiety reactions occur: "I'm well prepared. I'm devoted to my position. I want to talk to these people about it. I know I will feel better once I start to talk." And he will most likely be correct. Trembling hands, quivering voices, and dry mouths tend to disappear as the speech progresses. Perhaps by the end of the speech you will wonder why you were so upset over what has proven to be a rewarding experience.

Speech Anxiety Will Ruin the Effect of the Speech

One reason so many of us dread speech anxiety is that we believe we would be far superior as public speakers if we could approach each speech with calm assurance. There are some performance areas where this notion applies. For example, I recall an instance many years ago when as a clarinetist I entered a high school music contest. I was so overwhelmed with fear shortly before my perform-ance that my dry mouth generated more sour notes than harmonious tones. Of course, I didn't win. My fear had reduced my music to a series of squeaks and squawks.

Fortunately, this analogy does not necessarily hold for public speaking. *In fact, speech anxiety actually has the potential for enhancing your effectiveness as a public speaker.* Why? It takes a great deal of energy to make a speech. Not only do we have to talk for a sustained period of time, usually 20 to 30 minutes, but we have to enlarge or exaggerate many of our conversational speaking traits. Usually we must talk more loudly, gesture more forcefully, move more fre-quently, and vocally accentuate our ideas more vigorously. Among other things, communication anxiety produces *increases in available energy.* You need this energy for effective speech making (4). With the help of this extra energy you can move more briskly, gesture more forcefully, and project your voice more vigorously. In short, you can use your fear energy to create a more dynamic presentation. How you choose to use it will of course depend upon you. But what is important here is that you recognize that speech anxiety does not doom your speech to failure. Rather, it can equip you in such a way that you will actually perform more effectively. If you doubt the truth of this advice, recall that some of the world's most renowned public speakers have experienced great difficulty with speech anxiety. Included among them are Cicero (who wrote books about oratory and was known as one of the great orator's of his time), Abraham Lincoln, Winston Churchill, and William Jennings Bryan. Not only does this list demonstrate that one can excel as a public speaker while experiencing fear, but it should also reassure you that when you feel anxious about speechmaking you are in excellent company.

The Audience Is Hostile

Most audiences are friendly. This does not mean that they will love you no matter what you say. Nor does it imply that they will agree with you before your speech is over. "Friendliness" here simply means that they are willing to give you a chance. No one has bolted the doors. They have chosen to spend their time listening to you. Moreover, anyone in the audience who has ever given a speech knows that it takes a certain amount of courage to stand behind the podium and talk. Experienced speakers are no strangers to speech fright. Sixty to 75 percent of them admit to some anxiety on most speaking occasions (5). So they understand your position. They may take issue with some of your ideas or even heartily disagree with your proposed solution. But most audiences will be polite and sympathetic. Rarely do audiences throw eggs, rotten tomatoes, or barbed comments. Even difficult or offensive questions or comments come after rather than during the speech, at which time you are more relaxed and capable of dealing with them.

STRATEGIES FOR HANDLING SPEECH ANXIETY

Being Well Prepared

When and if speech fright strikes, there is no better psychological mechanism for dealing with it than to be able to say honestly to yourself that you are well prepared. You have sensitively selected a topic of interest to you as well as to the audience. You have thought reflectively and gathered information when needed. You have carefully organized your speech so that it is clear, coherent, and unified. You have practiced; that is, you have said it out loud several times, timing it and getting the reactions of friends or watching yourself in a mirror. You have done your homework: within reasonable limits you could not have done more. These kinds of thoughts are reassuring and even liberating. When you genuinely believe that you have prepared well, you might reasonably conclude that your delivery will reflect that preparation and the audience will sense that you have labored to bring to them something worthy of their time and attention. And you should remember that the audience has some responsibility too. Just as you hope to speak well, they need to listen carefully. The responsibility for the outcome of the speech event is shared. When you know that you have conducted yourself responsibly during the speech preparation process, you have every right to approach the speech's delivery with confidence.

Anticipating the Speech Situation

There are times in life when it is rather pleasant to be surprised. Before or during a public speech is probably not one of them. What happens if you thought you were addressing a few dozen people and it turns out to be a few hundred? Suppose you planned a very formal presentation and you arrive only to discover a half dozen people clad in jeans and sweat shirts? Or imagine you had planned to speak for half an hour and you are told right before the speech that you have fifteen minutes? What do you do? If you are thinking that these represent unusual and exaggerated situations, you are mistaken. Each of these represents a speaking crisis I have encountered during my years as a public speaker. They could happen to you as well. How do you avoid such occurrences?

First, you need to gather as much preliminary information about the audience and speaking situation as possible. Whenever someone asks you to make a speech, try to obtain most of the following information:

1. Suggested topics?
2. Audience makeup? (Here you need a better answer than "the Bedford League of Women Voters" or "the Bloomington Lions Club." You need to know something of anticipated *audience size, age, sex, and their reason for asking you to speak.*)
3. Location of speech?
   a. Size of room
   b. With or without podium, blackboard, etc.
   c. With or without microphone
   d. Location of building (possibly obtain map)
4. Time constraints?
5. Questions to follow speech?
6. Meeting time? Anticipated length of entire meeting?

If you are asked to speak near your campus or your home city, it is wise to visit the speaking site in advance. See for yourself where you are to speak and the facilities available. If possible, you might even stop by during an earlier meeting of the group so that you can see the audience and observe how they react to another speaker. Gathering this kind of information allows you to anticipate a good deal about your speaking environment so you can plan accordingly. In this manner your surprises are more likely to come in the form of an unanticipated check or gift representing the audience's gratitude. And those are surprises you can live with!

Exercising for Relaxation

When you are about to make a speech and you feel tense and nervous, some simple exercises may be done to facilitate relaxation. Of course, it would scarcely be appropriate for you to throw yourself on the floor and start doing push-ups or deep knee bends. There are, however, some more subtle exercises that should prove helpful. One excellent way to relax is to *breathe deeply*. While concentrating on breathing is simply a form of distraction, deep breathing allows you to take in a large quantity of air, giving you a good supply of oxygen and the potential for vocal control. Deep breathing here refers to abdominal or diaphramatic breathing. It's the kind of breathing babies do naturally. Later, many of us switch to chest breathing, in part, because we think it is more subtle; that is, we don't like to see our abdomens heaving in and out. Unfortunately, with chest breathing we take in less air and so we breathe more frequently. Singers and actors know about the importance of diaphramatic breathing for good vocal support. If you aren't sure which method you are using to breathe, place your hands at the bottom of your rib cage on either side. If you are breathing properly you should feel considerable outward movement whenever you inhale. You can usually correct poor breathing habits by concentrating on pushing your abdominal cavity out as you inhale. Even if you have difficulty learning to do this kind of breathing on a daily basis, with a little practice you should be able to do it prior to a speech to help you relax.

Another form of exercise some speakers find useful is *isometric movements*. Isometric exercises involve tensing and then relaxing a muscle of your choice. You might, for example, clench and unclench your fists, press your legs together firmly and then relax them, or squeeze the palms of your hands together as if you were trying to flatten a piece of clay. A variation of this is to push your leg, arm, or foot against some immovable object, such as a wall, table, or even the podium. After you have pressed firmly, release the muscle, relaxing as completely as possible. The principle behind isometric exercise is that by inducing tension and focusing on that tension for a few seconds, you are then better able to relax not only the exercised muscle but the rest of your body as well. Isometric exercises are subtle and can normally be performed in front of an audience without being noticed.

Finally, a useful form of mental exercise is *active listening*. Rarely do you make a speech under circumstances where you arrive, jump up and talk, answer a few questions, and leave. More likely, you are part of an ongoing program, dinner, or business meeting. Other people will speak both before and after you do. If you listen to them it will help you think about something other than your own anxieties. Equally important, you might learn something you need to know, something about the audience or the occasion. You might discover, for example, that they are celebrating a special anniversary or that they have been honored for some community project they sponsored. As a way of acknowledging your respect for them and their accomplishment, you might want to refer to this fact during the early moments of your speech.

SPEECH FRIGHT IN PERSPECTIVE

Understanding speech anxiety is an important step toward being able to manage it. We say "manage it" rather than "eliminate it" because moderate and controlled anxiety can help you improve your speaking effectiveness. As you begin making speeches and trying out some of the techniques you are reading about in this book, remember that each speaking situation will be unique. On occasion you will encounter previously unimagined problems. The microphone may fail. The podium may collapse. Your glasses may break or your earring fly off. *The point is that you have* some *control over your public communication activities but you do not have* complete *control.* While this may sound frightening, it is also one of the things that makes public speaking so interesting.

Above all, you need to take to each public speaking event a sense of humor. Prepare well, do your best, be flexible, listen to others—but if something goes wrong, look for the humor in it. What do you do if a dog wanders into the room in the middle of your speech? What happens if the fire alarm goes off (an unfortunate fire drill)? What if, heaven forbid, you lose your place for a moment or two? In most of these instances you can smile, perhaps comment briefly, and then go on with your speech. Even if you feel that your entire speech is a complete flop, you have probably learned a few things about public speaking. Perhaps you learned what not to do, but at least you learned. (And chances are you weren't as bad as you thought.) Concentrate on what you learned. Look for the humor. Get ready to have another go at it. Public speaking is, among other things, a great adventure.

EXERCISES

1. The next time you are asked to make a speech, do all of the following:

    ____ Gather preliminary audience information (refer to pages 4–6).
    ____ Examine the speaking environment (through questioning or, preferably, an actual visit).
    ____ Select your topic and plan your speech with the above constraints in mind.
    ____ Practice your speech at least *five times.*
    ____ Before you practice, go through breathing exercises.
    ____ Also before practice, try some isometric exercises.
    ____ During at least two of your practice sessions find someone to listen to you; solicit his or her feedback.
    ____ Practice once or twice in front of a mirror.
    ____ If you "blow it" (losing your place, for example), start over again immediately. Don't fret or dwell on errors.

―――― Use bodily movement and gestures as you speak (to help you burn up nervous energy).

―――― Say to yourself at least five times before you speak: "The audience is *not* hostile!"

2. Join a Toastmaster's Club or a Student Speaker's Bureau. Gain as much experience as possible as a public speaker. The Toastmaster's Club is especially good because you can learn about public speaking while speaking to your friends, a clearly sympathetic audience. The more often you speak, the more you will learn about your own speech anxiety and the less anxiety you will experience.

3. Find people in your college or community whom you consider to be fine public speakers. Talk to them about public speaking. Ask them about their experiences with speech fright. It will be comforting to learn that those you admire and consider to be excellent speakers have had to deal with speech anxiety. Furthermore, you may pick up some helpful hints about how to deal with your own anxiety symptoms.

4. Whenever you make a speech, have faith in yourself. As soon as the speech is over, sit down alone and reflect on what you have learned and how you hope to improve in the future. No matter how brilliantly or pathetically you think you've performed, it is crucial that you learn to view your speechmaking as growth experiences and that you examine those experiences with an eye toward the future.

NOTES

1. A great deal of research during the past two decades has focused on communication apprehension. See, for example, James C. McCroskey, "Oral Communication Apprehension: A Summary of Recent Theory and Research," *Human Communication Research* 4 (1977), pp. 78–96; Phillip G. Zimbardo, *Shyness: What It Is and What to Do about It* (Reading, Mass.: Addison-Wesley Publishing Co., 1977); and Myron W. Lustig and Stephen W. King, "The Effect of Communication Apprehension and Situation on Communication Strategy Choices," *Human Communication Research* 7 (1980), pp. 74–82.

2. Carl Rogers, *On Becoming a Person* (New York: Houghton Mifflin, 1961).

3. Theodore Clevenger, Jr., "A Synthesis of Experimental Research in Stage Fright," *Quarterly Journal of Speech* 45 (1959), pp. 135–139.

4. J. P. DeCecco and W. R. Crawford, *The Psychology of Learning and Instruction: Educational Psychology* (Englewood Cliffs, New Jersey: Prentice-Hall, 1974). In this work they point out that moderate anxiety enhances performance.

5. See, as examples, E. D. Wrencher, "A Study of Stage Fright in a Selected Group of Experienced Speakers," M.A. thesis, University of Denver, 1948 and R. S. Ross, "Survey of Incidents of Stagefright," unpublished research, Wayne State University, 1961.

chapter 5

Choosing the Subject of the Speech

CHAPTER OBJECTIVES

After studying this chapter you should be able to:

1. List and explain the perspectives from which you should consider topic selection.
2. Conduct a self-inventory.
3. List potential sources of subject information.
4. Choose an appropriate subject for a public speech, given a particular audience and situation.
5. Conduct preliminary research on the subject.
6. Focus the subject appropriately.

INTRODUCTION

Your phone rings. An unfamiliar voice asks, "Is this Michael Williams?" You respond affirmatively and the voice continues, "This is Ralph Peterson from the Jeffersonville (your home town) Lions' Club. I ran into your father the other day, who told me about your college activities. He said that you're a journalism student and that you've been on the college newspaper staff for two years." Again, you respond affirmatively. He continues, "Well, we're putting together our fall programs, and I thought it might be nice to have you come back to Jeffersonville and tell us about your experiences as a journalist. Would you be interested in doing that? If so, let's talk about a possible date." Let us assume that you agree to make this speech. Where will you begin? What, in fact, is your topic? Do you have enough information about it as a result of your studies and work experience or do you need to gather more? What specific aspect of the subject will you deal with? What do you think your audience wants to hear?

As you can see, there are many questions you must face before you can actually begin to work on your speech. How you respond to these questions is crucial because everything you do thereafter will be based on the subject you choose and your perceptions of audience expectations. For many speakers, topic selection presents a major problem. Even when a general topic has been suggested, as was the case in our opening illustration, there remains a certain amount of ambiguity. In fact, given the general subject requested in the introduction, you might choose several different specific subjects. Here are some examples:

Journalism Ethics
The Most Interesting Stories I've Written
Why A Career in Journalism Is So Attractive
Freedom of the Press in the 1980s
The Role of the Media in Influencing Public Opinions
How To Write a Good Newspaper Article
Important Journalists of the Twentieth Century

And we could go on with this list for some time. Clearly, subject selection is not as straightforward as it sometimes seems. Even when it appears that you have been assigned a subject, what you have been given, more accurately, is a subject universe from which you must choose a particular topic. Many speakers deal with the correct general subject; yet their specific treatment is so far removed from the audience's expectations and needs that they fail. The purpose of this chapter is to assist you in choosing the best topic for the particular speaking situation in which you find yourself.

PERSPECTIVES FOR TOPIC SELECTION

Sometimes you will receive a speech request that is especially concrete. You may be asked to describe a leadership training workshop you just attended, demonstrate an exercise program that you have developed, persuade an audience of the direct relationship between food additives and hyperactivity in children, or convince a group of students to join the Student Foundation. In that these kinds of topics are rather clearly specified, you have a good idea of what is anticipated by your audience. More commonly, however, you will have to spend some time choosing the particular aspect of a topic that you wish to pursue. In these cases it is useful to consider potential topics from several different perspectives.

You, the Speaker

As you begin to think about topic selection, you should begin with yourself. You, after all, are the person who has been asked to make the speech; therefore, your views must be of some interest to this audience. Sometimes, in fact, an audience will be so eager to hear a particular speaker they will simply say, "We don't care what you talk about as long as you will agree to be our speaker." This sounds like a marvelous compliment and, indeed, a great ego boost for the speaker. Unfortunately, if you take that kind of remark at face value, you may have some real problems. What the audience really means is, "We've heard you speak before or we've heard about your speaking reputation or we know you're good—*we trust you to talk to us about something we will enjoy." The more unspecified the topic is, the more control you have over the situation; but you also have a great deal of responsibility.*

In your quest for topics you should follow this general principle: *select a topic about which you already have some knowledge or expertise and in which you have a continuing interest.* Of course, your background and present student status suggest several potential topics. But before jumping into obvious choices, why not begin by taking a self-inventory to examine a wider spectrum of your interests and experiences. Use the chart appearing in Figure 5.1 to assess potential topics growing from your life experiences.

Suppose, for example, that you are presently attending an elite eastern university, but before going to college you lived and went to school in the poverty belt of Appalachia. That might be of great interest to some audiences whose children attend poorly staffed or racially troubled schools. Perhaps even before you attended college you successfully managed your family's business for several

---

Self-Inventory for Public Speakers

1. Education background (be sure to include anything interesting and/or unusual)

2. Jobs held (skills developed during jobs)

3. Childhood experiences of note

4. Traveling

5. Special training

6. Organizational affiliations (social, civic, religious, professional)

7. Hobbies/"outside" interests

8. Subjects on which you are widely read

9. People who have influenced your thinking (including family, friends, writers, world leaders, etc.)

Figure 5.1

months. Many audiences would like hearing about the factors related to your success. Maybe you've held interesting part-time jobs. Perhaps you have a pilot's license, have worked in the Peace Corps, or have acted in several plays. Maybe you studied abroad or traveled with a political candidate or were stationed in Germany while in the army. Possibly you were reared in foster homes or had a narrow escape from drugs as a teenager. Maybe you are a returning student and the mother of three small children. You may be extremely active in your church, the Big Brothers and Big Sisters program, or the Campus Crusade for Christ. Maybe you are a chess buff or a computer wizard or you helped build your family's home. Possibly you are widely read in science fiction, gender roles, or American history. Among those who have influenced your thinking are John F. Kennedy, Woodrow Wilson, and your father.

As you go through this exercise, you should discover a broader range of potential topics from which you might choose. Not all of your interesting "tidbits" will be appropriate for public speeches. Most audiences would not care to hear about your views on science fiction or your personal experiences with drugs unless you are presently a science fiction writer or are employed by a drug abuse center. In many cases the best topic will be related to your ongoing experiences, often related to your career pursuits. When you choose a topic related to what will likely be your life's work, you are dealing with something to which you have an enduring commitment, a depth of knowledge, and growing experience that are typically absent from your hobbies and casual reading pursuits. When audiences perceive you as experienced and knowledgeable, they will view you as being credible. One of the greatest assets you can have as you go into any public speaking situation is to know that your audience believes in your credibility. That's why your topic selection depends not only upon your interests and perceptions but upon those of the audience as well.

The Audience

It is possible to write great poetry or compose fine music without having any particular audience in mind. Speeches are different. By their very nature they seek an audience response. You can no more make an effective speech without an audience than you can win a tennis match without a partner. In the latter instance, you can bat balls around and practice your serve on your own, but without someone to receive your serve there can be no game. Likewise, with public speaking you can select a topic of great fascination to you, string together pretty words, and say them all out loud in an empty room. But you are not making a speech until you present your ideas to an audience. Thus, it is crucial that you consider your intended audience throughout the topic selection process.

Whenever you are asked to make a speech, learn as much as you can about your audience. If possible, seek the following basic information:

1. Audience size
2. Age range and average age
3. Gender makeup

4. The name of the organization asking you to speak and its general purposes and philosophies
5. Educational level/range
6. Socioeconomic level/range
7. Religious beliefs
8. Political leanings
9. Topics this group has enjoyed in the past
10. Names of speakers who have recently addressed this group
11. Other relevant values

You may not need to seek all of this information for every speech. If you know, for example, that given the topics you are considering, religious and political beliefs are irrelevant, then omit those questions. If, however, you are planning to talk about women and the draft, you must know the sexual composition of your audience. Or suppose your topic is related to nuclear energy; you should know something of the educational level of your audience so you can make judicious decisions about scope and detail. In almost every case you ought to know something of anticipated audience size since large audiences suggest the need for greater formality.

It is especially helpful to discover what topic the group has responded positively to in the past. You might learn, for example, that they have appreciated topics with an economic dimension, such as how to purchase life insurance, strategies for balancing the federal budget, and the impact of inflation on higher education. Even if your topic is unrelated to economics, you might conclude that you should treat your topic in a sensible, no-nonsense manner.

Finally, obtaining the names of former speakers can be invaluable. After all, they can give you insights that you probably will not get from the program planner. They might tell you that the audience seemed bored, reticent, fun-loving, or intense. Of course, you must remember that their judgments represent personal perspectives, no doubt colored by their perceived success or failure with the group. Even so, these kinds of perceptions can prove very useful. If you find out, for example, that a particular audience is often described as bored and listless, you might make a special effort to select a topic of extremely high interest value and as directly related to their immediate concerns as possible.

In assessing the audience's view of your credibility, you must also consider their attitudes toward your subject, for the two are related. An audience may think highly of you and yet hold an attitude in opposition to yours. Or, in contrast, they may know nothing of you in advance but favor the ideas you are advocating. Which is preferred? Probably the best position is to be a beloved person whose ideas stimulate, reinforce, and inspire the audience. Few of us are ever in that position, however. Moreover, what is best depends, in part, upon what you hope to do. If, for example, your objective is to get the audience to think reflectively, to question their own ideas, or to hear about some alternatives they have never before considered, then you may prefer an audience whose ideas are quite different from your own. What is important is that you *anticipate* audience attitudes so that you might select your topic with realistic expectations as to the response you are likely to encounter.

The Occasion

Audiences and speakers do not meet casually. Rather, they meet in the context of a formally acknowledged occasion. Sometimes audiences gather for the express purpose of hearing a speaker; hence, the speechmaking *is* the occasion. Certainly in a speech class speechmaking is the daily agenda. Outside the classroom, however, your speech will commonly be part of some other meeting, ceremony, or celebration. Being a commencement speaker is very different from talking to the monthly meeting of the Ladies' Literary Society. Not only do the audience members differ substantially, but the formality of the two occasions is scarcely comparable.

Most speaking occasions carry with them their own time constraints. Ministers typically talk for 20 to 30 minutes, college professors lecture for 45 minutes, and in your speech class, you may be given only 3 to 5 minutes. Expectations are important. If you expected to speak 30 minutes and you are told right before the speech that you have 15, that presents a real problem for you. Some business organizations, for example, meet during lunch and when 1:00 P.M. arrives members get up and leave, whether or not the speaker is finished! Hence, it is vital to determine time constraints so you can choose a topic that can be fully developed in the amount of time allotted.

Finally, if the audience is meeting for some special reason, such as an anniversary or honors day celebration, you need to be aware of that fact so you can mention it sometime during your speech. Like you, audience members enjoy being recognized and appreciated for their accomplishments. In expressing your knowledge of their meeting's significance, you establish an atmosphere in which the open consideration of your ideas can fruitfully occur.

Your Organization

Sometimes the job of making a public speech seems to be a rather lonely activity. You go through a great deal of work on your own and then you stand up by yourself and talk. However, in the minds of the audience you often represent not just yourself but also the school or organization with which you are affiliated. Some audiences have never met a representative of IBM, the United Methodist Church, Pillsbury, or State College before listening to you. They may assume, therefore, that you are "typical" of all those who go to your school or church or work for your organization. You may feel that this is absurd, but *it is important to recognize that as long as you are identified with an organization, you will be viewed not simply as an individual but as a representative of your school, church, company, or profession.* You have, therefore, a great deal of responsibility to reflect positively the organization you represent.

At this point several distinctions must be made. First, there is a difference between making a speech on your own and having your school, company, church, or student group ask you to represent their position to some audience. In the latter instance you must be very careful that you articulate the company's position clearly, whether or not that position is the same as your own. In the former instance, however, you have a good deal more freedom to discuss your personal views. Suppose, for example, that the college you attend is generally opposed to faculty unionization but you think it would be a good idea. In making a speech on this subject, you might wish to state your school's position and reasons for their position and then go on to explain your own point of view, acknowledging strengths and weaknesses associated with each.

Of course, some organizations are more tolerant than others in dealing with opposing points of view. Yet, most prefer that the individuals who represent them publicly express views that are reasonably compatible with the organization's major goals and values. For example, the academic community has long been recognized as an organizational environment that encourages freedom of expression. Even so, it is hard to imagine a university dean making a speech to some audience outside the university in which he would advocate tenure for all faculty members, the abolition of grades, or the right of faculty members never to do research. Such positions would probably be considered so deviant to the other members of the academic community that even if the dean were not fired, his social relationships would probably suffer appreciably.

Clearly, you need to consider the organization you are representing as you go about the task of selecting a speech topic. This is not to say that you are simply an outlet through which your school or organization communicates its views to the public. But the organization does provide some constraints and a framework in which you must operate. Thus, as you think about potential speech topics, consider these questions:

1. Is this topic of any concern to my organization?
2. What is my organization's stand on this issue?
3. Is its position public knowledge?
4. To what extent does my opinion differ from or resemble the organization's?
5. Am I being asked to speak for the organization, for myself, or for both? How comfortable am I with what I've been asked to do?
6. Might I deal with the topic by sharing information but without revealing a particular point of view?
7. How important is this issue to me and to my organization?

Once you have thought about possible speech topics in terms of your own interests, the audience's interest, the speech occasion, and the organization you are representing, you are ready to choose a tentative subject to begin to investigate. I say "tentative" because until you have thought about the topic in greater depth and discovered what information is available to you, you cannot be sure that this is the subject you should pursue. The most obvious example of this concern is represented by the college speech student who told her professor that she selected one topic over another because she couldn't find any books on the first subject in the library. This, of course, is often an easy excuse, but if it were true, it would represent a valid reason for topic elimination.

GATHERING INFORMATION

In examining any potential speech subject, you should begin by taking a personal inventory. What do you already know about the subject? Suppose, for example, that you have been working part-time at a crisis intervention center. Because you have been so successful, your boss has asked you to talk to a group of new volunteer workers about strategies you have found helpful. Possibly you are studying psychology and counseling as part of your college major and so have some formal schooling in the subject. You also have several months of excellent experience about which you may talk. However, you still need to conduct a personal inventory by asking yourself some of the following kinds of questions:

1. When did I first become interested in this subject?
2. How did I first become interested in it?
3. Why have I maintained my interest?
4. What is the breadth and depth of my knowledge?
5. What is my knowledge based on? Formal learning? Practical experience?
6. What kinds of personal experiences have I had with this topic?
7. What have I read about this topic? (List sources and authors.)
8. How dated is my information?
9. To what extent are my experiences limited? How might I broaden them?
10. What information gaps do I need to fill?
11. Where might I get additional information on this topic?

It is not uncommon for a speaker to have some experience with his subject; quite possibly, however, that experience is limited. Perhaps he has only worked at the job for a few weeks, has dealt with just one particular aspect of a problem, or has only studied something in school but has had no practical experience. Equally important are audience perceptions of the speaker's credibility. If you are a most learned master of your subject and have superb experience, but your audience does not perceive you as a highly credible authority, then you need to move beyond your own experiences to validate your ideas. In any case, you must begin by looking at what you know. Once you have determined the limits of your own knowledge and experiences, you are ready to begin to enlarge upon them.

On some occasions you may decide to conduct field research as a way of gathering information. Field research typically involves interviews or surveys. Suppose you think that most students in your college support intercollegiate athletics but you're not sure. You choose to conduct a *survey.* Surveys are good data collection devices in that they provide a breadth of response. If you do not have special knowledge about how to put together survey items, you might consult a statistics expert. When you administer your survey remember to choose respondents who are representative of the population to which you hope to generalize the results. It is also important that you select an adequately large sample and that you attempt to choose individuals at random. Some speakers are tempted, for example, to survey those people they know best, those they are sure will be cooperative, or those who are conveniently located. After all, if your college has 10,000 students and you only survey those 50 persons who are your friends or who live on your floor in the dormitory, you are in no position to generalize your findings to the whole student body.

Suppose you conduct your survey and discover that your initial perceptions about student supportiveness are correct; however, you are puzzled about some answers you received to two or three of the questions. For example, some expressed discontent with the undue emphasis the school places on football to the exclusion of other sports. Unfortunately, your survey doesn't allow you to discover the reasons behind such complaints. To learn more, you decide to *interview* several students. The disadvantage of the interview, of course, is that it is very time consuming. But it does allow you to seek explanations, to discover reasons, and to establish personal contact with your fellow students.

Whatever questions you intend to pose should be planned carefully in advance. Ask everyone the same basic core of questions, using varied follow-up probes depending upon individual responses. As you plan your questions for interviewing, take care that you do not phrase leading or loaded questions, ones that intentionally or unintentionally reveal your feelings. For example, you might be tempted to say, "I was disturbed to learn on the attitude survey that many of you were unhappy with our school's emphasis on football. Why do you view this emphasis as inappropriate?" Such a question reveals the attitudes of the interviewer and also puts the interviewee on the defensive. A far better question might be, "What do you think of the relative emphasis we place on different athletic events here?" This question does not point the way to the "correct" answer. Rather, it allows the respondent to choose her response and encourages positive and negative views equally.

Finally, you may wish to seek out written materials as you explore your subject. Those written documents may be right under your nose: daily articles appearing in the school newspaper or the college's published financial statement. Suppose, however, that you need to read widely on your subject, necessitating a trip to the library. There you will find abundant information on most topics. Your job is to locate it as expeditiously as possible. You might begin with the card catalogue, which lists authors, titles, and general subject areas. There are also a number of standard sources for locating reference works, such as *Basic Reference Sources, Guide to Reference Books,* and *The Guide to the Use of Libraries.* If you want to find particular articles appearing in popular magazines, check *The Reader's Guide to Periodical Literature.* Guides to articles published in professional journals include *Applied Science and Technology, Psychological Abstracts,* and *Business Periodicals Index.*

You may need to gather information on a recent news event. If so, examine *The New York Times Index.* Occasionally, you will need materials that pertain to official government records. *The Catalogue of the Public Documents of Con-*

Interviewers should plan and prepare their questions in advance before conducting an interview. Their questions should let the interviewee choose a response, not lead the interviewee to a response. (Photo courtesy of Art Stein, Photo Researchers, Inc.)

gress and of all Departments of the Government of the United States is a major comprehensive index of government documents from 1893 to the present. A helpful source of information for recently published books is *Books in Print.* A less complete work, but one that includes summaries, is the *Book Review Digest.* Whenever you are unable to find the kind of information you are seeking, ask a reference librarian for guidance.

As you discover relevant or interesting information, take notes. Undoubtedly you will devise your own note-taking system, but you might try using note cards so that later you can put together related items of information. Figure 5.2 demonstrates a simple, useful format for recording information on a note card.

FOCUSING YOUR SUBJECT

Once you have gathered preliminary information you are ready to focus your subject. First, you must decide what particular aspect of your topic you will discuss. Time constraints will influence this decision. You can deal with a much

Sample Note Card

Subject Heading:

------- Recorded Information -------

Source of Information:

Figure 5.2

broader aspect of a subject if you are speaking for 30 minutes than if you are speaking for ten. Begin, then, by examining your topic in relation to your speaking time. Next, you have to make a decision about the amount of depth you want to pursue. This will depend upon the kind of information you have assembled and the nature of your audience. If an accountant is talking to a group from the Big Eight accounting firms, he will probably choose in-depth coverage of a technical matter, such as an innovative auditing procedure. If, in contrast, he is addressing a local citizens' group, he might discuss pointers on how to prepare one's own income tax statement. Or if he were talking to a group of college students majoring in accounting, he might present a broad overview of different careers open to those with accounting degrees.

What is important for you to recognize is that the appropriate topic focus must be determined by the same factors that you initially considered in selecting the topic. What is too broad for one audience may be too narrow for another. A particularly technical presentation of such subjects as genetic engineering, management by objectives, multivariate statistical techniques, or nuclear power might be inappropriate for most audiences but perfectly acceptable for a group of experts in each area. *All speech subjects can be treated in multiple ways, with varying depth of focus. The focus you choose should reflect your knowledge, the audience's interests and competence, and the demands of the speech occasion.*

TOPIC SELECTION IN RETROSPECT

Most students of public speaking are eager to find a topic so that they can get on to the "serious business" of getting ready to make the speech. The point of this chapter is to convince you that the first item of business in speech making *is* topic selection. If you choose wisely, all subsequent steps in your speech preparation and delivery will be easier. If you settle for any topic or focus it improperly, then everything else will become more difficult. By taking your time during the topic selection phase, you will save yourself precious time later. Moreover, it is pleasurable to work with a subject about which one is genuinely enthusiastic. It is certainly enjoyable to present a speech to which the audience responds positively. Your chances of experiencing these positive outcomes will be greatly enhanced if you give serious attention to topic selection.

EXERCISES

1. Choose an audience to whom you might reasonably be asked to speak, possibly your class. Conduct a self-inventory to determine topics of interest to you. Then choose one that seems to be appropriate to this audience. Write a paragraph in which you explain the rationale for your topic choice.

2. Given the topic you have selected, start to collect information. Jot down personal experiences or relevant knowledge already in your possession. Conduct a survey or interview others if needed. Collect additional written information by examining materials available within your school's library.

3. Now make a list of potential aspects of the topic you might deal with, assuming that you have been asked to speak for 20 to 30 minutes. At first simply brainstorm, making a long list reflecting as many options as possible.

4. Choose the particular aspect of the subject that you presently feel would be most appropriate. Write a paragraph in which you discuss the rationale for the focus you have chosen.

chapter *6*

Selecting the Purpose of the Speech

CHAPTER OBJECTIVES

After studying this chapter you should be able to:

1. List and describe different speech purposes.
2. Distinguish among speeches that interest, inform, or persuade.
3. Understand the criteria for good purpose statements.
4. Write good purpose statements.

INTRODUCTION

Imagine yourself going to visit a friend who invites you to play a card game with him. He shuffles the cards thoroughly, arranges them into two neat stacks, and instructs you to draw a card from the stack closest to you. Since he doesn't provide further direction, you ask as you draw the card, "What do I do with this once I get it?" Reasonably enough, you want to know something about the object of the game. Without some understanding of the goal you are striving for, you cannot make sound choices about preferred ways of getting there.

The same is true of speechmaking. You must have a sense of purpose or direction in order to make intelligent decisions about effective strategies for accomplishing your goals. Many public speakers believe that once they have a topic they are ready to collect and organize information. Topics by themselves, however, do not suggest a goal or purpose. Suppose, for example, that you decide to talk about women pursuing nontraditional careers. How should you organize your thoughts and information? What kind of information should you collect? Statistics? Testimony? Illustrations? How should you deliver the speech? The answers to these kinds of questions can best be determined on the basis of your response to a more fundamental question: What do you hope to accomplish? You might want to give an informative speech, for example, in which you discuss the kinds of nontraditional jobs that women presently occupy and the kind of training they need for being successful in these occupations. Perhaps you prefer to convince the audience that certain career stereotypes about women are no more than myths. Or maybe you will choose to persuade the females in the audience to consider pursuing nontraditional careers, like engineering or veterinary science. Of course, in making these kinds of decisions you are becoming more specific about the particular focus of your subject, but you are also beginning to look at the direction or goal orientation you want your speech to have.

In a sense this entire book is about purpose. You are asked to look at each chapter in terms of objectives you might hope to accomplish by studying and practicing the materials and exercises presented. In this chapter, however, you are encouraged to begin your speech preparation with a thorough consideration of potential objectives or purposes. You will probably want to consider a wide range of alternative purposes before choosing the one best suited to your interests and knowledge and the needs and interests of your audience. That process of examining alternative purposes is critical; yet, it is one often ignored by speakers who make speeches without having the vaguest idea of what they are trying to accomplish. Unfortunately, these speakers usually leave behind them bewildered or even angry audiences who ask themselves and each other, "What's the point?"

DIFFERENT KINDS OF SPEECH PURPOSES

Suppose you are a candidate for vice president of the student body. You have been asked to address a rather large and influential group of student leaders from sororities, fraternities, and dormitories just a few weeks before the election. The fraternity president who asked you to address the group simply indicated that he wanted you to "tell the group about some of your ideas." Although you tried to get him to be more specific, he dodged your questions by saying that they'd be glad to hear you talk about anything relevant to the election. You decide you really want to address these students and you feel that it is important to impress them favorably. But how might you impress them? What do you want to accomplish? The obvious answer is that you want to win their votes. In that case, you might use a strategy of trying to demonstrate the superiority of your views over those of your opponents. Perhaps you should argue on the basis of your years of experience in student government. Or you could argue on the basis of your double major in business and political science. Maybe you should make reference to the fact that 25 years ago your father was elected president of the student body here at your own school.

As you reflect on the options, it occurs to you that the students who are to compose your audience are very bright. They know your university and they have their own private concerns. What they really need from you is an honest, concise statement of your position on the two or three controversial issues that ultimately will decide the election outcome. Thus, you start to view your speech as being more informative than persuasive, and you set out to inform them of your views on the campus parking dilemma, student representation on faculty committees, and rising tuition. Your strategy will be to explain to them your position on each of these issues and something of the evidence and reasoning that led you to feel as you do.

This example illustrates several important principles about selecting purposes. *First, the most obvious speech purpose may not be the preferred one or the one upon which you will ultimately settle.* Whenever a purpose seems too obvious, you should ask yourself, "What other purposes might I attempt to achieve?" Even if you decide to go with your original idea, the process of considering alternatives will broaden your perspective on the subject of your speech. *Second, you should think of your speech purpose in terms of the kind of audience response you hope to obtain.* In the illustration above, for example, you decided you want the audience to make an honest choice based on accurate information. Your goal, then, is to provide them with thorough information about your views so as to assist their decision making. This goal is quite different from convincing them that they should vote for you. *Third, once you have a clear notion of your intended goal, you are then in a position to think about judicious strategies for accomplishing it. It is impossible to have a strategy without an objective.* The more specific your objective, the better your chances of choosing a good strategy for getting you there. If, for example, you know that you want to give a persuasive speech against the John Birch Society, that is not as specific as setting out to persuade your classmates to sign a petition against allowing the local John Birch chapter to use university meeting facilities. *What is important is to ask yourself what kind of specific response you want from your audience.* You may want them to think reflectively, vote, sign a petition, buy a product, or endorse your candidacy. Thus, your purposes may be varied, but you still must be able to identify them.

Although speeches may have numerous specific purposes, there are three major general purposes that most speeches set out to achieve: *to interest, to inform, or to persuade.* Suppose, for example, that you are putting yourself through school by working part-time for an insurance company. You decide you want to convince your classmates that they should purchase their automobile insurance from you. Clearly, your general purpose is to persuade. But in order to be persuasive you will have to tell them about different insurance options and probably spend some time comparing and contrasting the insurance your company has to offer with that available through other firms. In this case your primary purpose is to persuade, but you will also devote a great deal of your speech to providing information. In most instances these general purposes work interdependently.

The Speech to Interest

The notion of "being interesting" in a public speech can mean many things. In the most fundamental sense, every speech must strive to interest the audience. No speaker can be informative or persuasive if he or she is incapable of presenting arguments and ideas in interesting ways. As with other speech purposes, however, you must consider the potential interest value of your speech in terms of your audience. That is, no speech is interesting to everyone. Rather than searching for a subject of universal interest, then, it is far better to focus on the particular audience you are about to encounter. For example, consider the college professor who teaches courses in social psychology. If she were asked to speak to a community group about her field, she might choose to speak about "social games" that people commonly play, both consciously and unconsciously, and some of their destructive consequences. This kind of subject should be interesting to most general audiences since it gives them useful insights into their own behavior and their interactions with others. If that same psychologist were to speak to a group of fellow psychologists at a national convention, however, she would probably elect to discuss the implications of a social learning theory or methodological innovations in her own research. Scholars pursuing similar research would find these latter topics to be quite interesting. Should the psychologist be so foolish as to reverse the topics, however, neither audience would be particularly interested.

An obvious question following from the preceding example is: What determines audiences interest? In general, audiences will respond with interest to:

1. *Information they perceive to be relevant to their lives.* If you happen to be a 30-year-old single parent, a Catholic, and a high school teacher, then you would probably be interested in hearing a speaker talk about the traumas/responsibilities of being a single parent, the Pope's view of abortion, or teachers' unions. The same subjects might be of little interest to you, however, if you were a 70-year-old Jewish grandfather.

2. *Information they perceive to be useful.* As a senior in college you are motivated to learn about job hunting strategies in a way that an established executive is not. For you, the subject is useful.

3. *Information they perceive to be startling/unusual/new.* Every semester college speech teachers hear speeches on the dangers of smoking cigarettes, the necessity of wearing seat belts, and the need for curbing inflation. Certainly all of these subjects are worthy of our consideration. The problem, however, is that speakers rarely say anything about these topics that hasn't been said numerous times before. Thus, the interest value is much lower than that of more unusual topics, such as training women to be astronauts, Japanese robots on the assembly line, or televised religious programs.

4. *Information they perceive to be worth knowing/repeating.* Not everyone would agree on what is worth knowing. However, some subjects are more substantive and thought-provoking than others. General topics dealing with various aspects of religion, politics, marriage, child rearing, education, and the economy usually seem more worthy of our attention than "how to avoid getting sunburned," "why hot dogs are bad for you," or "the fun of scuba diving."

   5. *Information they perceive to be amusing/entertaining:* Most people associate the "speech to interest" with the "speech to entertain." Indeed,
   many speakers give talks designed primarily to be entertaining. The
   comedian/after-dinner speaker is a case in point. When listening to
   speeches to entertain, audiences do not expect to gain valuable information. In fact, most assume that information shared in this context is as
   likely to be fabricated as it is to be authentic. The audience is there to
   enjoy; the speaker is there to amuse. While this may sound like a speaking venture enjoyable to both speaker and audience, speeches to entertain can be among the most difficult and demanding. By their very nature
   these speeches depend on the use of humor. Not everyone is capable of
   being humorous in a public speaking context. Moreover, humor, to be
   well received, must be carefully adapted to the audience. If you tell a joke
   and no one laughs, your failure is clear to everyone. Bob Hope is an
   excellent example of a comedian who adapts his remarks to his particular audience. Mr. Hope often appears on college campuses and is received with great enthusiasm. A few years ago Mr. Hope entertained at
   Indiana University. Interestingly, most of his jokes centered on the
   specific campus and community of Bloomington. He used the names of
   the university president, the basketball coach, and he often referred to
   specific fraternities and campus functions. His student audience loved
   him.

As you read over the preceding list of ways to be interesting, you probably
noticed that there are several different dimensions to the concept of interest. Subjects that are relevant and/or useful may be in no way amusing or startling. Topics
worth knowing or repeating are more likely old than new and rarely entertaining.
What you must decide then is *in what sense* you hope to interest the audience.

If you decide that the general purpose of your speech is to interest the
audience, you then must concern yourself with thinking more specifically about
the response you hope to achieve. Let's assume for a moment that you have had
the misfortune of selling encyclopedias door-to-door for two or three summers.
Your experiences have taught you a great deal about successful sales strategies,
but you have learned equally as much about ineffective sales techniques. Many
of your experiences have been humorous, so you decide to talk about "Seven Sure
Strategies for Getting the Door Slammed in Your Face." In this instance you
might phrase your specific purpose in this way: "In this speech I hope to amuse
the audience with my account of sales blunders." Or you might say, "I want the
audience to enjoy hearing about my account of sales blunders."

How will you know whether you achieve your purpose? Very often you will
not know for sure. It is difficult to be certain that an audience has been informed,
for example, as a result of listening to your presentation, unless you plan to give
them a quiz when the speech is over. When you make a speech to entertain or
amuse, however, you will find it much easier to judge your success. Although
listeners are very skilled at feigning feedback responses, as I discussed in Chapter
3, most have some difficulty acting genuinely amused over the course of an entire
speech. With these kinds of speeches, then, you can judge your success by watching for smiles and listening for laughter. If your purpose is more focused on

generating interest or enthusiasm than amusement, then you may have to look for head nods, facial expression, and other signs of real attentiveness.

The Speech to Inform

A second major purpose toward which you might direct your speaking efforts is to be informative. Whenever you choose to give an informative speech, your major purpose is to gain audience understanding. Often you will attempt to enlighten the audience regarding something they do not already know; that is, you will give them what you believe to be new information. Or you may decide to take a familiar topic and present it in a new light. Take, for example, the topic of smoking hazards mentioned above. Only a short time ago it was discovered that not only do cigarette smokers put their own lives in jeopardy, but they also present a health hazard for those who live with them. Even though "smoking hazards" appears to be an over-used topic, the speaker might provide new information about this subject by focusing on the health problems created for others who live with smokers. As I mentioned earlier, it is very difficult to be informative without at the same time being interesting. Those subjects perceived by audiences to be useful, timely, relevant, or worth knowing are usually the ones about which they would like to learn more. And when the audience wants to learn, your job of providing information becomes much more manageable.

As with other speech purposes, the specific informative purpose you choose will be determined by your assessment of the audience's needs, interests, and expectations. *Again, an understanding of your concrete purpose is vital because that purpose will guide you in choosing a pattern of organization, kinds of supporting materials, and even how you will deliver your remarks.* Consider, for a moment, a young doctor who is doing her internship at a renowned medical center. One of her jobs is to make a presentation to patients who are about to undergo open-heart surgery. Her purpose is to describe what will happen to them before, during, and after their surgery. She wants them to understand what is likely to occur, to be able to identify many of their experiences as normal, and to feel reassured that they are going to survive their surgery and be healthier individuals because of it.

Because of the situation in which these listeners find themselves, the usefulness and relevance of the topic are apparent. Hence, this doctor doesn't have to worry about making her remarks interesting. Part of her presentation will be persuasive in that she wants her audience to be convinced that they are going to move through their operations normally and successfully. Her primary purpose, however, is to gain their understanding. She is assuming that they have a right and a need to know what they are going to experience during this critical time in their lives. Some of the information she presents may even be a little frightening. She must tell them, for example, that the breathing tube inserted through their throats and into their lungs throughout the surgery and for at least 24 hours after the operation will prevent them from verbally communicating with the nurses and doctors or even from swallowing. Although this news may sound intimidating, she is convinced that it is better for them to know about it and anticipate it rather than wake up in the recovery/intensive care unit only to discover for the first time that they can neither talk nor swallow.

As with all informative speeches, this young doctor's remarks must be clear and accurate. She may choose, for example, to organize her remarks chronologically, discussing the procedures in the order they will encounter them. To insure clarity during her discussion of surgical procedures she will probably need to use some visual aids depicting the heart, its arteries, and valves. She might use slides or even pass out additional reading materials after the presentation is over. To be clear she must avoid using medical jargon as much as possible, and she must plan time for questions after her formal remarks to allow patient-listeners to pursue matters of individual concern.

In many ways this extended example is typical of informative presentations. Typically, whenever you choose to make an informative speech, you will need to:

1. Describe, define, or explain an idea, procedure, or process so as to gain understanding.
2. Concentrate on clarity and accuracy.
3. Consider using visual aids to enhance clarity and interest.
4. Reserve time for questions.

The Speech to Persuade

The final major purpose toward which your speaking may be directed is persuasion. In a sense we might argue that all speeches are persuasive. When you explain how to play chess, describe how to operate a new computer, or discuss the causes of increased thefts on campus, you are hoping that the audience will accept your view of the information presented. Even so, many speeches are far more directly and overtly persuasive. When, for example, you argue for the acceptance of a new book rental system, advocate a new grading scheme, or try to convince others to vote for a particular political candidate, you are speaking persuasively. Not all persuasive speeches are the same, however. Some persuasive speeches attempt to *stimulate,* some to *convince* or *change beliefs,* and others to *incite to action.*

Sometimes public speakers are asked to speak to a group of listeners whose needs, attitudes, and values are virtually identical with their own. When Ronald Reagan addressed a group of powerful House and Senate Republicans concerning the advantages of his economic package, he was facing a friendly, supportive audience. You might wonder why one should even give a persuasive speech in this kind of situation. Reagan's speech in this instance is a clear example of the speech to stimulate, a speech designed to make a group of supporters even more enthusiastic, more committed, more convinced that they should endorse his views.

Sometimes a speech to stimulate is aimed primarily at the individual listener. The minister who preaches to his congregation that there is a need for them to translate their Christian principles into social action is probably hoping to see them become more involved in worthy volunteer community projects. He knows or believes that they already agree with him. His goal, then, is to stimulate their already present beliefs so that they might become even more committed as Christians. Similarly, the Democrat who addresses a group of Democrats about the need for party support, the basketball coach who discusses with fans the need for their backing the team, or the GM executive who talks to the board about the virtues of GM's products are all speaking to stimulate.

Sometimes persuasive speeches intended to stimulate also have a goal that extends beyond the immediate audience. When Reagan talked to Republican supporters, for example, he probably did not view increasing their enthusiasm as his only persuasive purpose. Rather, he believed that their increased commitment would lead to their more active advocacy on behalf of his economic plan. By stimulating the immediate audience, he hoped to solicit the support of those reluctant or opposed with whom this audience might associate. The typical public speaker is not in a position to speak directly and persuasively with everyone from whom he might desire support. But if he can stimulate a group of dedicated, enthusiastic followers, these individuals may also become advocates so that the speaker's purposes ultimately may be achieved.

Many persuasive speeches seek directly to convince audiences or change their beliefs. The would-be persuasive speaker might ask an audience to believe that abortion is morally wrong, that capital punishment is no deterrent to crime, that divorce should be avoided at all costs, or that advanced academic degrees are important. When we argue so as to convince an audience, we make the assumption that the audience needs convincing, that is, that the audience either has no particular position or that their position ought be changed.

By their very nature speeches to convince involve changing the status quo. Hence, they represent a very demanding task. Most listeners, like us, have formed their attitudes over a period of years. Their attitudes have been influenced by the ways they have been socialized, what they have experienced, and what they have learned from parents, peers, school, and the media. Attitudes that have formed over the period of a person's lifetime are not readily susceptible to change, especially following exposure to a 5-, 10- or 20-minute one-shot presentation. *That's why it is important to be realistic about what one might hope to accomplish in a persuasive speech.* Usually it is possible to encourage the audience to begin thinking along the lines you are advocating. It is certainly possible to move an audience from a position of neutrality to a position relatively favorable to the one you are endorsing. If, for example, you are discussing the issue of busing with a Ladies' Literary Society, a group of middle-aged to elderly women who are primarily interested in becoming informed about controversial social issues, you may find it relatively easy to convince them that busing is positive for purposes of racial balance. The same thesis would not be so readily accepted, however, by a group of parents whose children presently walk to a school a few blocks from home but would have to ride on a bus for 45 minutes if busing were instituted in their city. Clearly, when audiences have strong attitudes or are personally involved with the topic, the job of convincing them to think differently, to change their beliefs, is not an easy one.

The last type of persuasive speech is the speech to incite to action. In giving this kind of persuasive speech, the speaker seeks more than a positive feeling or a change in attitude; *he seeks a behavioral commitment, an action demonstrating the person's position.* In making a speech to actuate, you might ask an audience to sign up for a course, sign a petition, cast a vote, give blood, join an organization, or join you on a picket line. Inciting audiences to action is perhaps the most difficult of all the persuasive goals. It is one thing for listeners to start to change an inner feeling about a subject, or even to articulate positive views; it is quite another for them to give of their time, talent, or money on behalf of the cause you are advocating.

Most of the time we assume, and rightly so, that people's attitudes and values guide their actions. But this is not always the case. Many individuals have definite positive or negative attitudes toward particular issues; yet, consciously or unconsciously, they have no intention of ever doing anything about them. One reason for this seeming inconsistency is that most of us have some needs and values that are more important than others, many of which come into conflict from time to time. For example, suppose you have a rather neutral attitude toward the idea of giving blood to the Red Cross. Then you hear a young hemophiliac (a bleeder) make a speech in which he articulates a strong and moving appeal for giving blood to save lives like his own. Moved by his empassioned plea, you decide that giving blood really is something that most good citizens should do. You may even chide yourself for having never done it before. During the question and answer period, you comment that you fully agree with the speaker. You point out that the sacrifice is relatively small, considering how life-saving your blood can be for others. A week later you see an announcement in your local paper indicating that the Red Cross bloodmobile is in town for a week and donors are solicited. What will you do? Have you really been persuaded to the point that you will act as the speaker advocated?

Perhaps you feel that the response is straightforward: of course, you would give blood! Strangely enough, however, a few years ago an experiment that tested this very situation found that audience members were quite reluctant to commit themselves to action. Specifically, while the majority reported being convinced that the speaker was correct and endorsed the view that giving blood to the Red Cross was important, over 80 percent of those with such attitudes refused to sign up to give blood when the opportunity immediately followed the speech (1). Why the inconsistency? First, in a sense, "talk is cheap"; that is, it is relatively easy to check on an attitude questionnaire that you think something is a good idea. It is quite another to commit your time to doing it. *Thus, when we ask people to act we are usually demanding that they make a stronger commitment, which, frankly, some are not prepared to make.*

Equally important is the notion of conflicting needs and attitudes. In this instance, for example, a listener might reason: "I'd like to give blood; I think it's important, but I am afraid to do it. It probably hurts. What if I pass out? Maybe I need more information about how I will be affected before I decide definitely to do it at this time." Clearly the desire to give others something they need and the personal need to avoid pain are coming into conflict. Time may also be an issue. This is where rationalization plays a major role. One might reason: "I do intend to give blood, but my schedule for the next month is already impossible. I'll do it sometime in the future, as it is not possible for me to work it in right now." Some people who think this way follow through later; others simply never get around to it.

Whenever you make a persuasive speech with the intention of inciting an audience to act, remember that most behavioral commitment will require some sacrifice from them, or at the very least, some risk. They may have to set aside their personal needs, quiet their fears, make financial sacrifices, rearrange their already impossible schedules, or put their reputations on the line in order to support your cause. Of course, listeners are capable of responding in these ways, but for many it is a more difficult kind of response to make than merely acknowledging their belief in your cause. When you make a speech to actuate, you will

A calm, rational, and persuasive speech is usually needed in order to encourage someone to sign a petition. (Photo courtesy of Jean-Marie Simon, Taurus Photos.)

need to find ways of confronting these conflicting needs and diminishing the obstacles they present. In later chapters we will deal with potential strategies for arguing effectively under these conditions.

CONCLUDING GUIDELINES

This chapter has focused on speech purposes. In discovering your speech's purpose, you are setting the goal and by so doing, laying the groundwork for all that will follow. When you formulate your purpose statement, check it against these guidelines:

1. *What is the primary purpose of the speech?* To interest, inform, or persuade? In what sense do you hope to be interesting? What kind of audience understanding do you hope to gain? What kind of persuasion are you aiming to achieve?

2. *What is the specific audience response you are looking for?* Examples: "I want the audience to enjoy my discussion about scuba diving." "I want my audience to understand how to purchase scuba equipment intelligently." "I want my audience to sign up for a scuba trip to the Bahamas."

3. *Is your purpose realistic?* In a 20-minute speech you cannot acquaint your audience with the history of music in America, though you might discuss the contributions of a particular musician. It is inappropriate to discuss long-range investments with a group of senior citizens, but discussing community services and opportunities for retired people would be quite meaningful.

4. *Is your purpose clear?* If your purpose is vague, both you and your audience may experience a good deal of confusion. If you say, for example, "I want my audience to understand genetic engineering," that is no more specific than saying that you are going to talk about generic engineering. Again, you must return to the issue of what you want your audience to do. Perhaps you want them to learn about some of the most recent innovations in genetic engineering, or you want them to become convinced that genetic engineering is unethical, or to sign a petition of concerned citizens against future experiments with this growing practice in your state. These latter purposes reflect a clear conception of the kind of audience response you are seeking.

EXERCISES

1. Examine the following list of speech topics:

Seat Belts
Tax Reform
Advertising
Inflation
Alcohol

Government Regulation
Textbook Censorship
Divorce
Buying a Home
The Cost of Food
Natural Childbirth
Purchasing a Car
Conflict
Capital Punishment
Balancing the Federal Budget
Presidential Candidates for 1988

Choose any three of these topics and then select an imaginary or real audience to whom you might deliver a speech concerning these subjects. Write at least three purpose statements for each of your chosen subjects. Consider each of these as alternatives you might realistically pursue. Make sure they are realistic, clear, and are focused on audience response. Put a check by the one you prefer for each topic and state the reason why.

2. Examine the following purpose statements. Put a check by the ones that are good. Put an X by the ones that are poorly written. Write a sentence or two in which you indicate why they are poorly written and rewrite them to improve their quality.

"I want to talk with the audience about child rearing practices in early America."
"I want the audience to understand how to purchase meat wisely."
"I want the audience to sign a petition in favor of the new library."
"I want the audience to be amused by my account of mountain climbing."
"I want the audience to know about income tax evasion devices commonly practiced by political figures."
"I want the audience to think about the difficulties of the large business."
"I want the audience to join this church."
"I want the audience to like hearing about the importance of speech communication."

NOTES

1. Patricia Hayes Bradley and John E. Baird, Jr., *Communication for Business and the Professions* (Dubuque, Iowa: Wm. C. Brown Co. Publishers, 1980), pp. 266–267.

chapter 7

Supporting the Speech

CHAPTER OBJECTIVES

After studying this chapter you should be able to:

1. Understand the importance of collecting supporting evidence.
2. Identify different kinds of supporting evidence.
3. Discover evidence appropriate for supporting your assertions.
4. Test evidence against criteria to determine its quality.
5. Define basic reasoning processes.
6. Identify reasoning fallacies.
7. Discuss ways of enhancing your credibility.

INTRODUCTION

Suppose that as a college senior you have secured an internship in an excellent department store chain in the east. Your internship is in the area of fashion merchandising. You want to make a positive impression on the woman for whom you work since she has the power to offer you a full-time job at the conclusion of your internship. Not long after your approval you notice that the only persons who frequent the women's clothing departments in your store are middle- and upper-class, middle-aged and elderly women. Although there is a "Junior Ms." department, you note that the sales there are lagging, with fewer customers coming in even to browse. This is very disconcerting since the store is located in a shopping mall near many subdivisions where the primary female population is under thirty-five, and many are teenagers. After a quick preliminary investigation, you discover that other stores in the area emphasize their junior and young misses line while maintaining a sizable clientele among the population you are presently serving. You realize at once that some changes need to be made in your store's present purchasing practices but, since you are only an intern, you also recognize that you will need the cooperation of your immediate supervisor and other upper-level managers to instigate any change. Moreover, if you are successful in your persuasive efforts, your career prospects might brighten appreciably. You decide to put together a proposal for oral presentation at the next sales staff meeting advocating major changes in your store's fashion emphasis, especially arguing for some expansion of the "Junior Ms." division.

Given a speaking situation such as the one just described, where do you begin with your speech preparation? You already have a topic and a purpose. How should you proceed? Since your speech is to be a persuasive one, you need arguments to support your point of view. You must be able to articulate your reasons for advocating the changes that are needed. Equally important, you need supporting evidence to substantiate your reasons. Suppose you argue, in this manner: "We need to enlarge our Junior Ms. department. Not only will this result in increased sales within that department but it should improve sales in other women's departments as well." What you have done here is make an assertion; *but to be compelling your assertions need to be accompanied by evidence.* In this case you might add: "Last year the Vanity Fair made the same kinds of expansions I'm suggesting. Not only did their sales improve by close to 60 percent in the targeted department, but general sales among other women's departments in the store increased by 10 to 25 percent." Whether this is "good" evidence will depend upon several factors, including the source and accuracy of your statistics, whether the store you are using for purposes of comparison is truly comparable to your own, and how these increases compare with those experienced by other stores that did not make similar expansions.

In this chapter we will examine one of the most important steps in your speech preparation process—collecting evidence to enlarge, develop, and support your views. Good evidence can give life to arguments, making them more memorable. Evidence can take many forms, including statistics, illustrations, comparisons, examples, and testimony. Evidence does not stand alone. In fact, we usually are interested in examining evidence so we can draw some conclusions from it. In the latter part of this chapter I will discuss reasoning, including common reasoning fallacies. Finally, I will focus on strategies for enhancing your credibility. First, however, let us examine the evidence.

EVIDENCE

Once you have committed yourself to making a speech and know both your topic and purpose, you can begin to think about what you hope to say, the points you want to make within your speech. Regardless of your speech's purpose, you will be articulating several ideas, contentions, and propositions throughout your speech. You might make this assertion, for example: "We need to revitalize our scholarship program here at the University." On the basis of this assertion alone your audience would be unable to determine whether your argument was valid or not. To convince the audience that your point is a good one, you need to support it with evidence. Evidence is the body of fact and opinion pertaining to a subject. In most of your speeches you should use several different kinds of evidence. Some kinds of speeches, such as technical reports, rely heavily on statistical evidence, often presented with the assistance of visual aids. But informative reporting may also be enhanced by the use of examples, comparisons, and the opinions of experts. Therefore, it is probably best to assume that for most speeches you will use several different kinds of evidence.

Fact as Evidence

Much of the evidence you collect will be factual; that is, it will involve the relatively objective description of something without interpretation or judgment. We make assertions about what we view as reality. If our view of reality is accurate and verifiable, then it is factual. In collecting factual information it is important to seek *reliable sources* and to look through different sources to make sure we are finding *consistent* factual information.

You ought to be able to look in more than one place and find a consistent factual account of the number of people that voted for Reagan in the last presidential election, the unemployment rate for the first six months of 1983, and the major causes of early blindness. Whenever you discover inconsistencies, you should carefully examine your sources for bias or possibly conclude that there are different approaches to explaining a particular phenomenon. In the latter case, you should not try to present such information as factual. Some doctors might say, for example, that premature blindness is caused by vitamin deficiencies, by muscle strain, or by overexposure to intense light. Others may contend that such blindness is predetermined genetically and little can be done to prevent it. These conflicting opinions constitute theories, but they are not facts and should not be presented as such.

Facts are needed in most speeches and are a potentially compelling form of evidence. Compare the following assertions, the first presented without facts and the second supported with facts.

> "Most students in this college are pleased with the quality of the education they are receiving." (without facts)
> "Last year a student survey revealed that over 80 percent of our students are "extremely satisfied" with their educational experience here. Some areas that were the most positively perceived were: the quality of teaching encountered in the classroom, cultural events available to students at drastically reduced costs, computer facilities, and social opportunities. Given these widely shared sentiments, it is scarcely surprising that only two percent of our freshman quit school last year, a statistic far below the national college average of close to 15 percent." (with facts)

Statistics as Evidence

It is almost impossible to present technical reports or propose changes without using statistical evidence for support (1). Yet, many people are intimidated by statistics, imagining them to be quite complicated and confusing. It is helpful if you simply look at statistics as a numerical method of handling large numbers of instances. If you exercise some care in selecting and presenting statistics, they can be perhaps the most precise and concise kind of information available.

Among the most important and frequently used statistics are measures of central tendency, more commonly known as *averages*. In using an average you are usually talking about what is most often encountered, common, normal, usual, or ordinary in the situation under investigation. However, not all averages are identical. Specifically, there are three different averages: the *mean,* the *median,* and the *mode.* Many people just assume that the words "mean" and "average" are synonymous. This is hardly the case. To obtain the mean, one must add up the results of cases in question and divide by the number of cases; thus, the mean is the actual arithmetic average. It is not, however, necessarily the best or the preferred average to quote. If, for example, there are extreme scores in the distribution of numbers, the mean will reflect a greatly distorted version of the real central tendency.

Consider the following array of numbers: 20, 22, 25, 18, 26, 29, 26, 21, 23, 24, 17, 19. Here the mean is 21.7, a sensible indication of that distribution's central tendency. But suppose the numbers being examined were salaries, as follows: $78,000, $67,000, $26,000, $22,000, $20,000, $24,000, $21,000, $19,000, $25,000, $28,000. Here the mean is $32,000. If you were going to work for a department with that salary distribution, would you expect to make $32,000? Of course not. You can see that the extremely high salaries in the distribution distorted the mean, causing it to be much higher than the true average.

If you have reason to believe that the mean would not fairly represent the central tendency of the distribution you are discussing, it would be better for you to use the mode or the median. The mode is the most frequent score and the median is the middle score. Both of these statistics are unaffected by extreme scores. In large distributions they are often quite similar. For practice, compute the mean, median, and mode for the following array of scores: 100, 96, 88, 56, 50, 50, 50, 51, 58, 44, 43, 42, 38, 52, 49, 52. Which do you think would be a preferred average to quote?(2)

Apart from averages, there are other issues that must be considered in using statistics. First, most statistics we quoted in speeches are inferential rather than descriptive. That is, they deal with probabilities rather than with observable facts. If you pointed out that "25 percent of all teachers in this country belong to a union," you would be using a descriptive statistic. If you observed, however, on the basis of your survey of several hundred teachers that "over 80 percent of all teachers are dissatisfied with their retirement plans," you would be using an inferential statistic. It is inferential in the sense that you sampled the opinions of some group you believed to represent the views of a larger group and you generalized from the small group to the large population.

The point to be made here is not that all inferential statistics are potentially suspect; rather, it is important to recognize that *whenever one generalizes from a sample to a larger population there is always some margin of error.* That margin may be quite small, perhaps one in 1,000, but it does exist. Whether the inferential statistics you select are sound ones will depend largely upon the size and representativeness of the sample on which your statistics are based. If you want to know how students in your school feel about a particular issue, you need to solicit the opinion of a cross-section of the entire college, including freshman through seniors, men and women, different ethnic and racial groups, and students representing business, the arts, engineering, and other fields. Moreover, if there are 4,000 students in your school, your sample size ought to approach 400 rather than 30 or 40. Inferential statistics based on adequate and representative samples are often excellent pieces of evidence.

Finally, statistics, like other forms of evidence, should be used only when they constitute needed support. No speech should be "padded" with statistics simply because they seem impressive. In addition, every attempt should be made to present the statistics clearly and meaningfully. Often it is helpful to translate the statistic into audience-specific terms. Instead of pointing out that a new school will cost seven million dollars, you point out that each taxpayer should expect a property tax increase of approximately $50 per year over a ten-year period. In this way the audience can comprehend what the personal impact of endorsing your proposal would entail. Finally, statistics change most rapidly. Nothing is more useless or boring than outdated statistics.

Opinions as Evidence

Earlier we defined evidence as the body of fact and opinion pertaining to a subject. While factual evidence involves objectivity and suspension of judgment, evidence of opinion is the actual application of interpretation and judgment to the facts. There are three different kinds of opinion evidence you might use: *personal opinion, lay opinion,* and *expert testimony.*

Regardless of the kind of speech you are making, you are quite likely to state your personal views from time to time. This is entirely appropriate for most topics. What you want to avoid, however, is over-reliance on your own opinions to the exclusion of using other kinds of support. Equally important, you need to ask yourself a fundamental question: To what extent am I perceived by my audience as being a credible source of information on this subject? If you have high credibility with your listeners, then your personal opinion may be the most potent source of support you could possibly use. If, for example, you are a dentist discussing teeth care, a company vice president talking about business, or a floor supervisor discussing robots on the assembly line, your personal opinions and experience should be highly regarded. But suppose you are a businessman preparing a speech on inflation, a political candidate getting her thoughts together on national defense, or a college student preparing to discuss the importance of getting regular exercise. These are cases where the audience has no reason to believe that your expertise is extraordinary; thus, you will need to go beyond your personal opinions and gather other kinds of support.

A doctor who specializes in radiology discusses a medical problem with her students. The doctor is regarded as a highly credible source due to her expertise. (Photo courtesy of Richard Wood, The Picture Cube.)

Another kind of opinion evidence is lay opinion. Suppose you wanted to argue that most students were dissatisfied with the food being served in the dormitory cafeteria. To support this argument you might cite the results of a poll you've taken in which you state that 85 percent of all students polled indicated that they found the food to be "extremely poor." You might further note that out of 5,000 students who eat in the dorms, you surveyed 500—an excellent sample. In this case lay opinion is good evidence to use because the matter being judged does not require the testimony of an expert, and your personal views would not suffice. Thus, *lay opinion is useful when you want to describe the habits, attitudes, behaviors, and needs of ordinary people.* Normally, you would collect information regarding lay opinion by conducting a survey or by interviewing.

The final kind of opinion evidence is expert testimony. Most of us are not such renowned experts in our own fields that we could not profit from quoting others of greater renown who happen to support our views. In some instances you might be able to combine different kinds of opinion evidence. To continue with the above example, you might point out, "I have been very discouraged by the quality of food in our cafeteria [personal opinion]. My poll revealed that 85 percent of our students rate the food as "very poor" [lay opinion]. And even the company dietician, Lois Peterson, revealed to me in an interview last week that she was not pleased with the quality of many of the products purchased by our college for use in food preparation. In particular, she objected to the quality of meats, fruit, and vegetables [expert opinion]." This is an especially good example of expert testimony because the school dietician is known to the audience and, more important, is in a position of being able to offer some insights into the reason for the poor food quality. Moreover, since we might even view her as a potential "hostile witness" in that we would expect her to feel defensive about the food issue (she shares considerable responsibility for its quality), her testimony becomes even more persuasive.

Whenever you decide to use expert testimony to support your views, you need to observe a few guidelines. First, make certain that the person you are quoting really is an expert in the area on which you are quoting her. Sometimes it is very tempting to use the name of someone simply because that person is famous. Television advertisers do this with great regularity. Larry Bird and Magic Johnson probably know no more about the virtues of 7-Up than we do; yet, their testimony is solicited because they are well-known athletes.

Once you have collected a good piece of expert testimony, you must then decide whether your expert is known by your audience. If there is any doubt, make sure you identify her. You might say, for instance, "Dr. Linda Hoffer, Head Nurse at the Cleveland Clinic's Cancer Care Center, has pointed out that the most fatal kind of cancer is cancer of the liver." That identifying phrase, "Head Nurse at . . ." is important. Without it, your expert's testimony does not help your argument because the listeners do not recognize her position and expertise. It is also wise to make your reference to an expert specific. Many speakers provide only vague references to their sources by saying, "Authorities in New York have noted . . ." or "One police officer pointed out . . . ." The problem with referring to experts in this manner is that listeners are uncertain about whom you are quoting. The "police officer" could be a rookie cop or the chief of police; "authorities" could refer to the police, the sheriff, the mayor and his staff, or any of a variety of city officials. Audience members who are really listening to the quality of your arguments probably won't be impressed with such vague references to experts. They may even question you after the speech as to the identity of your sources.

Finally, whenever possible, quote those individuals who have nothing to gain from the position they are taking. One would expect the president of General Motors to advocate purchasing GM products. Of course, those involved in the space program would support added government expenditures for space exploration. Certainly, the Democratic chairperson thinks you ought to support the Democratic Party. Although these individuals would be considered experts in their respective fields, quoting them does little to assist your cause because they lack objectivity. In short, *those people whose views you use to strengthen your own position should possess the same qualities of credibility that you yourself hope to demonstrate.*

Examples as Evidence

One of the most difficult problems public speakers face is trying to make general principles or abstract notions interesting and meaningful to the audience. One of the best ways of doing this is through the use of examples. Examples provide concrete frames of reference and by so doing interject life and meaning into the point you are making.

Examples can be either actual or hypothetical, elaborate or brief. *Actual examples* make reference to real events or people. In the example that follows, Karl Menninger, the distinguished lecturer and psychiatrist, uses an actual example as evidence:

> The fourth observation I want to make is that some patients may have a mental illness and then get well, and they may get even "weller"! I mean they get better than they ever were. . . . Take an instance familiar to all of you. Abraham Lincoln was undoubtedly a far more productive, a far bigger man, and a far broader and wiser man after his attack of mental illness than he was before. Prior to it he had seemed to fail at everything—in his profession, in politics, in love. After his terrible year of depression, he rose to the great heights of vision and accomplishment for which we all know him. And Lincoln is not the only one; there are many others, but he is a conspicuous one.(2)

If Menninger had desired, he might have noted the names of a dozen or so well-known people who had passed through some kind of experience with mental illness and had gone on to make significant accomplishments, rather than elaborate on the Lincoln example; or he might have combined the Lincoln illustration with other specific instances.

The other kind of example you might want to use is hypothetical. *Hypothetical examples* are ones that might reasonably or plausibly take place, but in using them you are not referring to an actual event or person. Although hypothetical examples are "concocted," they should not be unrealistic or distorted. The following is one such hypothetical example:

> Suppose you were assigned to a committee to deal with declining membership in your fraternity. Your committee's mission is to try to find out what some of the causes might be, make a report to the board of directors, and possibly suggest changes in the present situation. You come to the first meeting with great enthusiasm. You've given the problem a great deal of thought and you've even collected some comparative information. You arrive at the meeting only to discover that one member has called in sick, two arrive late, and the other three seem more interested in chit-chatting than in discussing the problem assigned your group. How would you respond? Would you be angry? Confused? Would you confront the other members directly or complain to your president? How would you feel about coming to the next meeting? Would you come prepared? When we have committee experiences such as these, most of us begin to think that working in groups is a waste of time.

Because examples are so easy to identify with, they can be a potent means of support. Even so, they must be used with care. Most of the time when we use examples, we are arguing that the example represents the general principle we are discussing. *Thus, one test of a good example is its typicality.* If you are talking about the reading habits of children, during your research you might run across an example of a nine-year-old boy who regularly reads *Penthouse,* "trashy" comic books, and other questionable materials. Of course, you would not use this example to illustrate the point that children's reading habits were impoverished these days, unless you had reason to believe that this child was in any sense typical. Since you would have no reason to believe this on the basis of one isolated example, this would not become part of your supporting material. Unfortunately, many public speakers abuse this principle of typicality. A speaker at a rally aimed at people interested in joining an organization that would allow them to go into business for themselves, for example, once made a speech in which he argued that the audience had every right to believe that this venture would make them quite wealthy. He cited two or three illustrations of members who, through their own businesses, had been able to give up their former dull jobs and live in luxury. These examples were very misleading in that he was holding this up as a typical, anticipated result of joining this particular organization. While his examples were actual, their typicality was open to serious doubt.

There are times when examples do not have to be typical to be considered worthy of use. Specifically, you need to make some judgment about the *significance* of the example you plan to use. The Food and Drug Administration must often grapple with this issue. Suppose, for example, the FDA discovers that a drug they are about to market resulted in lethal side effects for one person out of 20,000 tested. That one person could scarcely be considered typical, but in this case the outcome is so serious and significant that it warrants the generalization that the drug should not yet be marketed. Likewise, a plant supervisor might find that out of every 500 cars his plant produced last year three to five had a faulty suspension system, apparently caused by careless assemblage. This problem could result in the car instantly going out of control at speeds over 40 miles per hour. Again, such an important piece of evidence does not have to be typical. Because human lives are involved, even two or three of these instances justify some remedial action.

Comparisons as Evidence

One of the primary ways that we learn is through *comparison.* We compare the known with the unknown, the more familiar with the less familiar. Whenever we encounter a new problem, we compare it with similar problems we have experienced in the past. New jobs, friends, and concepts are compared with old ones. Thus, a good way to help an audience understand what you are talking about is to compare your idea to something with which they are quite familiar or experienced. You might compare the job of managing a company with the job of managing a family. You might discuss the architectural design you had in mind for a new city municipal complex by comparing it to one in a neighboring town with which you know the audience is familiar. Or you might compare a new book to one you know they have read. By using these comparisons you hope to enlighten, to make the unknown more familiar, and perhaps to make your audience less afraid of something you are advocating.

What is important to remember in using comparisons as evidence is that they are only useful or enlightening when they are justified; that is, when the events, people, or phenomenon you are comparing are adequately similar to warrant the comparison. In the following passage, Martin Luther King, Jr. compares American students' civil disobedience to instances where such disobedience was justly practiced by others.

> We must never forget that everything Hitler did in Germany was "legal." It was illegal to aid and comfort a Jew. . . . If I lived in South Africa today in the midst of the white supremacy law in South Africa, I would join Chief Luthuli and others in saying break these unjust laws. . . . Our nation in a sense came into being through a massive act of civil disobedience, the Boston Tea Party. . . . Those who stood up against the slave laws, the abolitionists, practiced civil disobedience. So I think these students are in good company. . . .(3)

Can the student movement of the 1960s really be compared to the other historic instances King cites? If so, the comparison is probably a good and compelling one.

Testing Evidence

Not all evidence is of equal quality. Collecting a great deal of information on a subject is not enough. As you read, talk with individuals, and ponder the information you've unearthed, you need to make judicious decisions about what should be included in your speech and what should be omitted. There are several criteria to use in testing evidence: *accuracy, recency, completeness,* the *reliability of the source,* and the *appropriateness for the particular audience.* Not all of these criteria need be applied to every piece of information, but most of the time using one or more of them will be helpful.

Accurate information is redundant and verifiable. You should, for example, be able to examine several independent sources and discover essentially the same information. When serious inconsistencies occur, you should question the accuracy of your sources. Suppose, for example, that you were preparing to make a speech on abortion. Among other things, you want to report on the attitudes of the American public toward the legalization of abortion. The first article you find reports a recent survey in which 90 percent of those sampled are strongly opposed to legalized abortion. You are surprised at this statistic and you decide to check it against other sources. As you continue, you find that most other sources report only about 50 percent opposition. Returning to your original source, you notice for the first time that the article appears in a publication sponsored by the Roman Catholic Church. As you reread the article, you begin to infer that most of those sampled in this survey are Catholics. You go with the 50 percent figure as being far more accurate, reflecting true population attitudes.

Next, you should strive for the most recent information possible. Most libraries, for example, have a periodicals room where the most recent magazine, journal, and newspaper articles are kept. You may want to consult these, as well as looking for information relevant to your topic in the slightly more dated publication listed in the *Reader's Guide to Periodical Literature* and other indexes mentioned in Chapter 5. Of course, recency would be a more important criterion with some topics than with others. If you were presenting a historic account of how your community was founded, you would need good historical references rather than recent information. But such subjects as economic trends, consumer demands, and productivity figures change so rapidly that in order to achieve any sense of accuracy you must use recent sources.

You should also seek complete information—not that you can ever know everything there is to know about a subject. However, in general the more complete, thorough, and well rounded your knowledge is on a topic, the better your speech will be. Completeness and accuracy are clearly related, for as you check for accuracy you will consult numerous sources, and in so doing you will make your evidence more and more complete. The completeness criterion can become especially important when, after your speech, you respond to the audience's questions. At that point you will be asked to go beyond what you have said in the speech, elaborating, clarifying, exploring other facets of the subject. Some speakers really know little more than what they have discussed during their 20-minute presentation. This becomes painfully clear as they struggle with questions, trying to rephrase what they have already said. If you have collected your information with a concern for completeness, however, responding to questions should give you a chance to reveal additional knowledge in your possession.

Another concern regarding evidence is the reliability of the source from which it is taken. Whether you have collected statistics, facts, or illustrations, the quality of the source from which you gather that information must be scrutinized. The example given above concerning abortion is fairly typical of the kind of problem you might encounter. A Catholic magazine is not a reliable source for America's views on abortion because it lacks objectivity. Even if the publisher is well intended, some bias may creep into his publications. Equally important, when you quote that kind of source to an audience they will immediately be suspicious that some bias exists. Hence, even if the information is sound, it may lack credibility for your listeners. In general, whenever you doubt a source's objectivity, trustworthiness, or competence, it is best to disregard the information and look elsewhere.

Finally, regardless of the objective quality of the evidence you find, it should not be used if it is not appropriate for the audience and the speech situation. Rarely should a human interest story find its way into a technical report. Yet, the same kind of evidence is a necessity in most sermons and political oratory. Thus, the kind of speech you are giving, the topic you've selected, and your perception of the needs and values of the audience should guide you in your selection of appropriate evidence. Some evidence is more inherently logical; it appeals to the audience's rational thought processes. Other evidence is more stirring, moving the audience emotionally.

Appealing to Audience Emotions and Values

Emotional appeals are intended to make audiences feel sad, happy, angry, guilty, proud, or sympathetic. If you want to get your audience excited about some cause, move them to action, or help them to become less complacent, you will have difficulty achieving those goals on the basis of logical appeals alone. *There is nothing wrong with using evidence that has a strong emotional appeal, as long as there is a rational foundation underneath this appeal.* To get people to act or to move them to change some policy, you often have to move their hearts as well as their heads.

As you try to move your listeners to action, you should never substitute emotional appeals for evidence and reasoning. You should always build your persuasive speech on a firm foundation of facts and logic. Discerning listeners will not be moved by your emotional appeals unless you can prove your case. Once you have presented convincing arguments, you can use emotional appeals to kindle your audience's feelings, engage their belief, and incite them to action.

One of the most common ways of appealing to listeners' emotions is through the use of *a moving story or illustration.* Discussing basic facts about child pornography, inhumane nursing homes, or poverty in the inner city is scarcely adequate. You need to use specific examples. In this way, the emotional appeal grows from the content of the speech itself. Sometimes *your language can also evoke emotional responses.* Such words as "cruelty," "terror," "murder," "nightmare," "political fanaticism," "thrills," "peace," and "passion" can contribute to a stirring speech. You must be careful if you choose to move your audience in this way, however. Sometimes this technique is simply too obvious. This is especially true if the barrage of passionate language is inconsistent with the rest of the speech. The audience may respond with amusement or even hostility rather than with fear or sympathy. Thus emotionally charged language must be used tastefully and with restraint. Finally, perhaps *the most powerful source of emotional appeal is your sincerity, commitment, and conviction as a speaker.* You cannot move an audience simply by using the right words and plugging in colorful examples. Audiences are amazingly good at detecting insincerity or apathy. If you are feeling the emotions you wish to arouse in your audience, then everything you say and the way you say it will reinforce your commitment and convey a compelling message. Consider the following example in which a young hemophiliac makes a poignant plea:

You might ask—but what can I do? What do you expect of me? The answer lies in the title of this oration: mingled blood. For all that boy needs is blood, blood, and more blood. Blood for transfusions, blood for fresh frozen plasma, blood for serum fractions. Not Red Cross Bank Blood, for stored blood loses its clot-producing factors. But fresh blood directly from you to him in a matter of hours. Your blood, dark and thick, rich with all the complex protein fractions that make for coagulation—mingled with the thin, weak, and deficient liquid that flows in his veins. Blood directly from you to the medical researcher for transformation to fresh frozen plasma or antihemophilic globulin. During those years, his very life is flowing in your veins. No synthetic substitute has been found—only fresh blood and its derivatives.(5)

In suggesting this course of action, the speaker is assuming that certain values exist in the audience and that they might be the kind of people who want to help others, who have some desire to be self-sacrificing—that they would feel good about making this kind of contribution.

In every speech you make, as you choose and focus the topic, fashion the speech's purpose, and collect the evidence to support your views, you must make a continuous assessment of your perceptions of the audience's needs and values. Some audiences are more secure than others; some desire love and belonging; others desire being held in esteem (6). For some listeners, habits are their most powerful motivators; that is, they are very committed to the status quo because they are used to it and comfortable with it. They are instantly opposed to any idea that seems to suggest change. Others have a strong need to feel they are making a contribution "to the world"; hence, they are "other-directed." In the exercises at the end of this chapter you will find an activity that will show one way to examine audience values and discover how to appeal to them in your speeches.

REASONING

Very few of us run around collecting evidence for the sheer fun of it. On the basis of the evidence we discover, we seek to determine whether our assertions are sound and worthy of our continued endorsement as well as the support of others. *Reasoning is the process of drawing conclusions from evidence.* Sound reasoning is not automatic. Not everyone examining the same evidence would draw the same conclusion from it. One individual might discover several instances of corrupt political practices and go on to conclude that most politicians are corrupt, while others might argue that these are merely isolated instances, proving nothing. Some psychologists study learning in rats and generalize what they learn to human beings and their learning behavior. Others feel that such a comparison is unwarranted.

Normally, our reasoning processes take one of several basic forms. *We are using deductive reasoning when we begin with a generally accepted premise and apply that premise to a specific situation or person.* A classic example of deductive reasoning (called a syllogism) might go something like this:

    A. All ministers are pious. (major premise)
    B. Reverend Smith is a minister. (minor premise)
    C. Therefore, Reverend Smith is pious. (conclusion)

Most of us do not think or talk this formally, but we often rely on informal deductive reasoning when trying to be persuasive. Suppose you advance this argument: "If you want to get a good job, you had better obtain a college degree." In a formal sense, you are really arguing:

    A. People who graduate from college usually get good jobs.
    B. You want to get a good job.
    C. Therefore, you should graduate from college.

Once you put your claims in this form, you should ask yourself two questions: First, are the premises true? And second, does the conclusion follow logically from the premises? In this case, the answer to both questions is yes. The speaker's conclusion—"If you want to get a good job, you had better obtain a college degree"—seems sensible.

Let's consider a different example now. Suppose a speaker makes this argument:

> **A.** People who drink alcohol usually have more friends (than those who don't drink).
> **B.** You want to have more friends.
> **C.** Therefore, you should drink alcohol.

As a careful listener, you know better than to accept this reasoning. First, the basic premise is doubtful; there is no evidence that drinking alcohol leads one to acquire many friends. Moreover, even if it happened that those who drank alcohol did turn out to have more friends than nondrinkers, there is still no basis for concluding that they made these friends because of their drinking behavior. It may be, for example, that people who drink are also friendlier, and it is their outgoing personal styles that have led to increased friendships. Whenever you use deductive reasoning in your speeches, make sure that you discuss the evidence upon which you are basing your premises. Only then will both you and the audience know whether or not your conclusions are sound.

Another process you may use is *inductive reasoning. When you use inductive reasoning, you examine a set of specific instances, or make a series of observations, and proceed to draw from them a general conclusion.* Here is an example:

> Fact 1: My sister is weaker than my brother.
> Fact 2: My mother is weaker than my father.
> Fact 3: My best friend is weaker than her boyfriend.
> Conclusion: Males are stronger than females.

As this example suggests, we use induction every day, often without realizing it. We point out, for instance, that Democrats are liberal, professors are boring, women are emotional, rock stars are weird, and politicians are corrupt. Most of these generalizations come from induction—from observing several examples of each type of person and drawing a general conclusion. When we allow these conclusions to become unthinking, rigid categories, as we discussed in Chapter 2, we are stereotyping.

Although we want to avoid stereotyping, as public speakers we cannot avoid reasoning inductively. For example, the speaker who argues that overexposure to loud music results in impaired hearing is basing her conclusion on specific examples of people who have had this problem. Whether or not she is right will depend upon the number of cases she has observed. Her correctness will also depend upon the quality of the examples she is using. Could the people to whom she is referring be ones who have had their hearing damaged in some other way? Is there any chance of hereditary hearing weaknesses? Are there any dramatic instances to the contrary?

Of course there is always room for error. *Conclusions reached on the basis of either induction or deduction are probable, not absolute.* Very few premises on which deductive conclusions are based are universally true. If we believe, for example, that most English bulldogs give birth to small litters, we will usually be correct. But the couple who predicted such an outcome for their female bulldog learned that "most" is not the same as "all" when their dog gave birth to seven puppies. Similarly, breeders will tell you, based on their experiences with hundreds of bulldogs, that there is no more gentle breed in the world; indeed, they hardly ever growl or bite. Even so, a particular bulldog viciously attacked his owner when she tried to pull away a stick on which the dog was gnawing. Clearly, then, we are dealing with probabilities, not certainties.

Beside deductive and inductive reasoning, we also often reason causally and by analogy. For example, a student might point out, "I had trouble with my classes last semester *because* I was under stress." Here the speaker is trying to establish a relationship between cause and effect. Whether or not the speaker's reasoning is correct will depend, in part, upon whether there might be other explanations for his poor classroom performance—such as difficult subject matter or competition with superior students. Moreover, some studies have actually shown that moderate stress can cause individuals to improve their performance. Thus, the speaker would need to show that his level and type of stress was, in fact, debilitating.

A final example of reasoning is by analogy. When we reason this way we compare two similar cases, arguing that what is true for one is true for the other. Say, for instance, you wanted to argue that your college should establish an institute for the study of ethics. Through your research you have learned that Case Western Reserve University in Cleveland, Ohio, has such an institute. In your speech you describe the Cleveland system and argue that if Cleveland could do it effectively, your school should also be able to. Whether or not your analogy is a good one will depend upon the similarity of the two schools. Are the administrators at your institution committed to making such an institute work? What are the available resources, both in terms of people and money? How would the students at your school view such a center? Is your school located in the kind of community that could support such a venture? As you can see, many questions need to be raised and answered before you can determine whether or not your analogy is sound.

Common Reasoning Fallacies

Many things can go wrong during the reasoning process, leading one to draw a faulty conclusion. The following are some common reasoning fallacies that ought to be avoided.

1. *Glittering Generality:* jumping to a hasty conclusion on the basis of inadequate or unrepresentative observations. This is perhaps the most common inductive fallacy. We observe a limited number of college

students, blue collar workers, Catholic sisters, or businesspeople, and we draw a sweeping conclusion about all others of the same kind or class. Once the generalization is formed, it is very difficult for us to admit to exceptions, as was noted in the discussion of stereotypes in Chapter 2.

2. *Faulty Analogy:* comparing two things, persons, events, or phenomena that are not similar enough to warrant the comparison. A skeptical manager might note, "It's silly to talk about letting workers make decisions about their own jobs. You might just as well talk about giving horse racing back to the horses!" The comparison between workers and horses here is scarcely justified. There might be perfectly good reasons why workers should not make some of their own decisions, but this analogy fails to discuss any of them.

3. *Faulty Causal Reasoning:* a fallacy that confuses a chronological relationship with a causal one. Simply because one event follows another in time does not prove that the first caused the second. Suppose that you performed well in high school and now in college you have continued to excel. Did your achievements in high school cause you to do well in college? In part this may be the case since the knowledge you obtained in high school probably created a foundation for what you are learning now. However, the relationship is not nearly so simple. In fact, the real causes of success in these instances are more likely to be your intelligence, self-discipline, and motivation. This example also illustrates another important point about causal reasoning: most problems and their outcomes have multiple causes. Too often we oversimplify, seeking single and simple solutions to complex phenomena.

4. *Guilt by Association:* the quality of an idea or the worth of a person or program being determined solely on the basis of its association with other ideas, persons, or organizations. For some people, any idea that comes from persons they dislike is bad. If you view yourself politically as very liberal, you might be tempted to discredit the views of Ronald Reagan, Barry Goldwater, or William F. Buckley, Jr. because of their conservative images. Much research has shown that we frequently rate an idea, painting, essay, or speech much higher if we are told that it came from a person we feel has high credibility than if it is attributed to a neutral or negative source (7). What is important is to focus on what is being said rather than who is saying it.

5. *Bandwagon Effect:* the endorsement of ideas just because lots of other people support it too. Although our parents once admonished us not to "follow the crowd," it is a temptation for many of us throughout our lives. Most of us prefer being with others who support our ideas, and especially if we are uncertain about a particular issue, we take great comfort in knowing that others agree with our perceptions. As a public speaker it is wise to avoid appealing to the audience on the basis of "everybody's doing it." Just because many other students regularly use illegal drugs is not a good reason for others to do so unless you can show how these students lives have been improved as a result of such ventures. Knowing that a lot of people support an idea or a product is one piece of information you might want to collect, but that knowledge is not terribly persuasive by itself.

6. *Circular Reasoning:* the use of arguments that go in circles, with no proof for the assertions advanced. Suppose, for example, a speaker asserts, "Jane Marshall is brilliant." You might ask, "How do you know?" He might then tell you, "She belongs to Phi Beta Kappa." Would you accept this argument? Does being in Phi Beta Kappa prove that one is brilliant? Of course not. Jane may be a hard working overachiever, very motivated, but of average intelligence. To demonstrate brilliance, however, the speaker might refer to her problem-solving ability, her communication skills, or her creative genius. Just because something appears in a good newspaper, the annual report of your company, or even the Bible does not prove that it is sound, accurate, or a good idea. To determine the quality of an idea one must examine its logical merit.

7. *Red-Herring Argument:* some speakers do not want an audience to examine the quality of their arguments. To throw the audience off the track they raise emotional, often irrelevant, issues aimed at gaining listeners' hasty support. A speaker arguing in favor of prayer in the public schools might assert, "The real issue here is whether we are going to allow atheists to determine what happens in our schools." Yet, those who oppose prayer in schools may be deeply religious persons who simply uphold the principle of separation of church and state. The issue is not atheism, but the speaker hopes to get support by reducing the situation to simplistic and largely irrelevant terms.

The fallacies we have just examined are not the only reasoning problems you may encounter, but they are some of the more common ones. By becoming familiar with them you should have a better chance of using evidence wisely and convincingly.

BUILDING CREDIBILITY

Most credible public speakers know how to select sound evidence and reach well-reasoned conclusions. A speaker's credibility is of utmost importance. Aristotle wrote that the speaker's ethos, or credibility, is probably his most potent source of influence.(8)

So far, I have implied that your personal credibility will be a function of your expertise or competence in relation to the topic you are addressing. That is true in part. There is more to credibility than competence, however. Generally, if your audience perceives you to be *competent, trustworthy, objective,* and *enthusiastic,* you will have high credibility in their eyes. Audiences tend to believe speakers who seem honest, sincere, well informed, and genuinely committed to their ideas. Certainly these dimensions of credibility are interrelated. We have little regard for the words of the sincere but incompetent. Nor are we impressed by the brilliant but deceptive individual. Objectivity is important in that we want to believe that the speaker is both knowledgeable about and has given fair consideration to several different points of view in formulating his own opinions. We also like to believe that he would be willing to listen to views opposed to his. Finally, we like speakers who are dynamic, in the sense of being enthusiastic about their ideas, without being pushy or aggressive. The public speaker with high credibility can usually argue very convincingly by using personal opinion.

What can you do to enhance your credibility as a public speaker? *First, you must recognize that even before you begin to speak, the audience will most likely have some impression of your credibility.* If, for example, you are known as an expert on nutrition and you are speaking on the need for a balanced diet, the audience's perception of your credibility should be quite positive. However, even if the audience knows nothing about you, they will begin to assess your credibility as soon as they see you. Your appearance courts. As I pointed out in Chapter 3, some audience members will be so focused on your appearance that they will scarcely listen to you at all. The way you dress is important, as is the way you walk, sit, smile, and shake hands. Looking professional (suiting your attire to the occasion and appearing neatly groomed) is also essential.

Finally, your listeners will gain some impression of your credibility based on *the remarks of the person who introduces you.* Some introducers do not seem to know how to make a good speech of introduction. They either say virtually nothing, leaving the audience to wonder who you are and how you got there, or they drone on and on about every detail of your professional (and sometimes personal) life. Typically, the individual who introduces you will be an officer in the organization you are addressing. Often he or she will collect information from you during dinner or right before you speak. To discourage this haphazard method of speech preparation, you might send your introducer pertinent information (geared toward enhancing your credibility) several days before you are to speak. Avoid sending a full vita. Introducers often have trouble picking out the

The person who introduces a speaker gives the audience the first impression of the speaker's credibility. The introducer should provide pertinent information that enhances the speaker's credibility. (Photo courtesy of Phyllis Graber Jensen, Stock, Boston.)

really crucial information from a long vita. One master of ceremonies became so frustrated upon receiving a speaker's eight page vita that he made copies for everyone in the audience! Not surprisingly, the audience was a little put off by this rather pompous method of introduction. Clearly, even before you begin to speak, you and those who introduce you can do much to either damage or enhance your credibility.

Fortunately, the initial impression is not necessarily the final one. *You can also do things during your speech to alter your perceived credibility.* Building credibility is a process that unfolds as you share your thoughts with the audience. The following are some techniques you might try:

1. *Establish common ground with the audience.* In general, audiences enjoy listening to speakers with whom they seem to have something in common. Whenever you can demonstrate values, concerns, or aspirations that you and your audience hold in common, you help your credibility.

2. *Build trust.* Normally, trust building is a process that only evolves over some period of time. Even so, you can often establish yourself as a trustworthy source of information on a particular subject by such techniques as self-disclosure (admitting that you are an alcoholic as you begin to discuss the problem of alcoholism) or by establishing your individuality (speaking as a minister who once seriously questioned the existence of God).

3. *If appropriate, reinforce your status.* If your introducer does her job well, you may not have to do this. If not, however, tasteful references to your experience, education, or position are entirely appropriate. Mention your experience with mountain climbing, supervision, student government, and so forth as you address each of these subjects. Obvious name dropping or repeated references to a prestigious award or position must be avoided.

4. *Support your views with evidence.* We have already discussed the importance of using evidence. In general, the better your evidence, the more the audience will perceive you as credible. This is especially true if you present evidence with which the audience is not already familiar. With hostile audiences, presenting arguments both for and against your position is especially effective.

5. *Strive for good delivery.* In the last chapter we will discuss in detail principles of effective delivery. Here let us simply note that if you can deliver your speech fluently and with apparent confidence, if you can sound sincere and committed to your ideas, you will go a long way toward establishing yourself as a trustworthy, competent, and enthusiastic source.

6. *If appropriate, use visual aids.* Visual aids are not necessary for every speech. If they make sense and if you want to take the time to prepare them, however, they can add color and interest to your presentation. Using relevant hand-outs or overhead transparencies highlighting your main points or the presence of other carefully constructed visual aids suggests that you went to some pains to prepare for the presentation. This implies you took the task seriously.

There is no standard way of building one's credibility. Each topic, audience, and speech situation presents its own set of obstacles to be overcome. No speaker is equally credible on every topic he or she addresses. In some instances your credibility may be almost automatic. In others, you may want to consider using all of the devices listed above. In most speaking situations even highly credible speakers nurture their image by establishing common ground, using evidence, and striving for excellent delivery. It is simply impossible for one's credibility to be too high.

CONCLUDING COMMENTS

Every step in speech preparation is important. None is more important, however, than the ones we have discussed in this chapter. How carefully and thoroughly you collect and use objective evidence and how soundly you reason and establish your credibility will determine the quality of your speech. Some speakers are so eager to get something down on paper and start practicing that they neglect the substance of their arguments. This is not to say that one cannot get by with such practices. Indeed, some speakers are amazingly successful in stimulating audiences with poorly developed arguments and numerous reasoning fallacies. Often these speakers get by because their audiences are so supportive and do not know how to think critically, or possibly because their delivery is outstanding. In the long run, however, and especially in dealing with intelligent and diversified audiences, the really effective public speaker will learn how to collect and use information judiciously and ethically.

EXERCISES

1. Choose a topic for a public speech, possibly one of those you worked with for the exercises at the end of Chapter 5 or 6. Make sure that you give careful consideration to the audience to whom you will deliver it. Examine the lists that follow. The first is a list of instrumental values reflecting the way people often think of themselves. The second is a list of terminal values, focusing on the kinds of goals many of us have for our lives.

From each list choose three to five that you think might be especially important to your specific audience.

Instrumental Values

Ambitious (hard-working, aspiring)
Broadminded (open-minded)
Capable (competent, effective)
Cheerful (lighthearted, joyful)
Clean (neat, tidy)
Courageous (standing up for your beliefs)
Forgiving (willing to pardon others)
Helpful (working for the welfare of others)
Honest (sincere, truthful)
Imaginative (daring, creative)

Independent (self-reliant, self-sufficient)
Intellectual (intelligent, reflective)
Logical (consistent, rational)
Loving (affectionate, tender)
Polite (courteous, well-mannered)
Responsible (dependable, reliable)
Self-controlled (restrained, self-disciplined)

Terminal Values

A comfortable life (a prosperous life)
An exciting life (a stimulating, active life)
A sense of accomplishment (lasting contribution)
A world at peace (free of war and conflict)
A world for beauty (beauty of nature and the arts)
Equality (brotherhood, equal opportunity for all)
Family security (taking care of loved ones)
Freedom (independence, free choice)
Happiness (contentedness)
Inner harmony (freedom from inner conflict)
Mature love (sexual and spiritual intimacy)
National security (protection from attack)
Pleasure (an enjoyable, leisurely life)
Salvation (saved, eternal life)
Self-respect (self-esteem)
Social recognition (respect, admiration)
True friendship (close companionship)
Wisdom (a mature understanding of life)

2. Develop a research strategy. Decide whether you need to interview people, go to the library, conduct a survey, etc. Then begin to gather materials. As your arguments develop and specifically as you collect evidence to support your views, return to the audience value profile you just constructed above. Ask yourself: "How am I going to relate this argument to the needs and values of my audience?"

3. After you have collected most of the evidence you think you will use, examine your evidence for

    a. appropriateness to this audience
    b. accuracy
    c. recency
    d. completeness
    e. source reliability

Also make sure that you have some *evidence variety* and that you are able to *identify* the *sources* of your *information* in a way that would make their credentials clear to the audience.

4. Given the topic you've selected, what techniques do you plan to use to enhance your credibility? Why?

5. Go to the library and find a recent issue of *Vital Speeches of the Day* (published by City News Publishing Co., Box 606, Southold, New York). Choose any one of interest to you. Respond to the following questions:

a. Who is the speaker?
b. Who is the audience?
c. What are the audience's values, needs, interests?
d. Does the speech have a clearly stated purpose? What is it?
e. What are the speakers main points or assertions?
f. How good is the evidence he or she uses to support them?
g. How many different kinds of evidence can you find?
h. To what extent do you agree with his or her conclusions?
i. Any reasoning fallacies?
j. What credibility building devices did the speaker use?

6. Examine each of the following. To what extent does the evidence and/or reasoning contained in each seem sound? Can you find any fallacies?

a. "Dr. John Smith pointed out that out of every ten employees surveyed eight support unionization."
b. "I think you can see the merits of the program I represent. My program is, after all, in the tradition of other fine Democrats . . . Woodrow Wilson, FDR, and John Kennedy."
c. "Our products are hopelessly outdated. All of our competitors have gone with the newer trim line. If we are to keep pace, we too must change."
d. "Deaths in Atlanta have reached 25. One authority noted that this is the most baffling and morally degrading case with which he has ever worked."
e. "Our salaries are really quite competitive. In fact, the mean salary here is about $22,000 compared with averages of $17,000 and $16,000 for our major competitors."

NOTES

1. Wilbur Samuel Howell and Ernest G. Bormann, *Presentational Speaking for Business and the Professions* (New York: Harper and Row, 1971).
2. Karl Menninger, "Healthier Than Healthy," in *Contemporary American Speeches,* eds. W. A. Linkugel, R. R. Allen, and R. L. Johannesen (Belmont, Calif.: Wadsworth Publishing Co., Inc., 1965).
3. Martin Luther King, Jr., "I Have a Dream," in *Contemporary American Speeches,* 3rd ed., eds. W. A. Linkugel, R. R. Allen, and R. L. Johannesen (Belmont, Calif.: Wadsworth Publishing Co., Inc., 1972), pp. 289–293.
4. See, for example, Dennis S. Gouran, *The Process of Group Decision-Making* (New York: Harper and Row, 1974). Gouran discusses these four, to which we have added a fifth, appropriateness.
5. Ralph Zimmerman, "Mingled Blood," in *Contemporary American Speeches,* eds. W. A. Linkugel, R. R. Allen, and R. L. Johannesen (Belmont, Calif.: Wadsworth Publishing Co., Inc., 1965), p. 200.
6. See Abraham Maslow, *Motivation and Personality* (New York: Harper and Row, 1954).
7. Theodore Clevenger and J. Matthews, *The Speech Communication Process* (Glenview, Illinois: Scott, Foresman, 1971).
8. Lane Cooper (ed. and trans.). *The Rhetoric of Aristotle* (Englewood Cliffs, N.J.: Prentice Hall, 1960), pp. 91–92.

chapter 8

Choosing the Strategy of Organization

CHAPTER OBJECTIVES

After studying this chapter you should be able to:

1. Recognize the importance of choosing a good organizational strategy.
2. List several different attention-getting devices.
3. Construct a speech introduction so that it contains both an attention-getter and an orientation phase.
4. Identify several different patterns for organizing speeches.
5. Choose an appropriate organizational strategy for a given speech.
6. List several different concluding devices.
7. Construct an appropriate speech conclusion.
8. Develop a speech outline according to outlining principles presented.
9. Construct appropriate transition statements to be included in the speech outline.

INTRODUCTION

One of your fellow students has just finished giving a speech urging you and your classmates to support the local Democratic candidate for mayor. He began by stating his purpose and then discussed the vices of his candidate's opponent. Next, he quoted the number of citizens who voted in the last election, focused on the position his favorite candidate takes on several controversial issues, and concluded by discussing this man's personal and professional background. At the conclusion of the speech you feel confused. The speech seemed to have a lot of good information: the speaker quoted local newspapers, citizens' surveys, and highly credible political figures to support his case. But you find it hard to sort through the speaker's main points. Somehow the speech just didn't seem to hang together. Yet, you can't quite put your finger on the problem.

Whenever you have the feeling that a speech is not "hanging together," the chances are good that the speaker has not succeeded in organizing his or her remarks effectively. Speeches can be disorganized in many different ways. Some follow no discernible pattern. Others include so much irrelevant information that the main ideas get lost in the shuffle. Still others contain no meaningful transitions, making the speech's logical progression obscure. Some are so complexly arranged that the speaker's purpose never surfaces at all.

Whatever the nature of a poorly organized presentation, the effect upon the audience is likely to be negative. Disorganized speakers usually appear to be poorly prepared. Thus, their credibility suffers. Listeners have difficulty learning from disorganized presentations. Moreover, when the speech is over they often feel confused and frustrated without really knowing why. It is easier for the average listener to point to stammering delivery or identify a weak argument than it is to pinpoint the problem with a disorganized speech. Yet, if the listener cannot follow the speech because, for example, the relationship between arguments is not demonstrated through good transitions, then the whole speaking venture has been wasted. Even well-supported assertions cannot compensate for a disorganized speech.

During the past three decades several researchers have examined speeches to see what effect, if any, organization might have on the audience's reactions to the speaker and the speech itself. These experts have discovered several interesting things. First, they found that clear organization is positively associated with audience understanding and retention. That is, disorganized speeches are neither understood nor remembered by the people who hear them. They also found that previews at the beginning of a talk, which quickly summarize the main points of the speech, and reviews, which summarize the main ideas at the conclusion of a speech, also help audiences to comprehend and remember (1).

Organization may also have a second effect: it may influence audience perceptions of the speaker's credibility. The disorganized speaker is often perceived as lacking competence, of not being willing or able to handle the material in an enlightening way (2). He may also be viewed as not having taken the trouble to structure the speech in a clear manner. This suggests that he doesn't really care. *Thus, a poorly organized speech is often viewed as evidence that the speaker is neither especially competent nor concerned about his speech. Hence, his credibility is severely damaged.*

Finally, perceptions of the speech's quality are also greatly influenced by organization. Imagine listening to a speech that has several good arguments, excellent evidence, and clear organization. Then imagine listening to the same speech, excellent in every regard except that the arguments are scrambled. How do you think you would react? If your reaction is fairly typical, you would give the second speech a much lower rating than the first speech (3). That is, disorganization can make good arguments harder to follow and relationships among ideas difficult to understand. The audience has to work hard to try to follow the point, and frustration often sets in. Under these conditions neither learning nor attitude change is likely to occur. That's why once you have completed the research phase of the speech preparation process, the next crucial step is to select an appropriate pattern of organization.

PATTERNS OF ORGANIZATION

Suppose you are going to make a speech concerning the parking problem on your campus. You have conducted a student survey, interviewed several people, and examined alternative parking systems at other universities. Thus, you have excellent information. How are you going to organize your material? Perhaps you should trace the history of the parking problem on your campus, pointing to the way that campus growth and development contributed to the problem. Maybe you should discuss student attitudes toward the parking dilemma and contrast those with the opinions of college officials in charge of planning and developing parking facilities. Or maybe you should describe the problem as you see it and offer alternatives being used by other colleges. The available patterns of organization may seem endless. How do you choose among them?

First, regardless of your subject, there are likely to be several different patterns of organization that could be appropriate. It is a waste of time, then, to try to guess what the "ideal" pattern might be. *Try instead to think of what seems logical, sensible, and clear in light of your purpose.* The last five words of the preceding sentence—"in light of your purpose"—are critical. The pattern of organization you select should be viewed as part of a strategy designed to allow you to accomplish your purpose. If your purpose in talking about the campus parking facilities, for example, is to help your audience gain some understanding of how the parking problem evolved, then you might choose a chronological pattern of organization, citing key decisions and events that led to the contemporary dilemma. If, in contrast, you want your audience to be convinced that a particular parking alternative is better than the present system, you could structure your speech by describing the problem as you see it, then examining several alternatives, and finally, offering support for the alternative you prefer. This pattern is a typical problem-solution organizational approach.

With every speech you should approach the task of organization by asking yourself, "What organizational strategy is most likely to help me gain the audience response I desire?" To answer this question, of course, you need to consider a wide range of organizational alternatives. Some of these alternatives follow.

Chronological Order

As its name suggests, chronological order is based on the progression of time or the sequencing of events. Some sample topics that might call for this organizational approach are: How the Student Movement Developed in the '60s, Key Events in the War of 1812, Paul Simon's Musical Contributions, How to Write a Simple Computer Program, or How to Make a Speech. I'm sure you can think of some other examples. Almost any topic that can be approached from an historical perspective lends itself well to chronological order. Similarly, explaining any process or procedure as a sequence of events suggests the need for chronological treatment. Chronological order is most frequently used in speeches intended to create audience understanding or in informative speeches.

If you choose to use chronological order, make sure that you select a limited number of points to stress. There might be 20 steps involved in making lasagna, but you need only highlight the critical ones (perhaps providing the complete recipe for audience members at the speech's conclusion). Tracing the contributions of John F. Kennedy could result in dozens of dates, each representing an important event. But as a public speaker you must recognize your audience's limited capacity to remember detailed information. Thus, it is far better to choose four or five really significant dates or periods of Kennedy's life and discuss those thoroughly than it is to mention 15 or 20 and have the audience recall almost nothing.

Spatial Order

Spatial order is based upon the relationship of things as they exist in space. We use this pattern often in daily conversation whenever we are asked to give someone directions. The fact that so few people are able to give really clear directions probably suggests that this organizational pattern should be planned very care-

The teacher of a Chinese cooking class organizes her presentation in a chronological order. She tells her students how to prepare a dish in a step-by-step approach. (Photo courtesy of Laimute E. Druskis, Taurus Photos.)

fully. A spatial perspective might be used to describe the floor plan of a new building, the development of the feminist movement as it progressed from one part of the country to another, the anatomical features of the eye or the heart, or the geographic features of southwestern states. Like chronological order, spatial patterns are typically used in informative speeches.

If you decide that spatial arrangement is appropriate for you, you will have to begin by grappling with the issue of which spatial approach to take (left to right, east to west top to bottom, clockwise, or the reverse of any of these). Whatever approach enhances simplicity and clarity is probably best. Spatially ordered speeches are usually most effective when accompanied by some visual aids. A representation of the human heart, for example, could be sketched on a blackboard, presented on an overhead projector, demonstrated with a three-dimensional model, or drawn and presented in hand-outs. We will consider some of the advantages and disadvantages of these different visual approaches later. The point here, however, is that clarity in spatial organization can often be accomplished by using visual aids.

Topical Order

To some degree topical order represents a catchall category. Speech materials that do not lend themselves logically to any other pattern of organization can often be arranged topically. *When you arrange your ideas topically, you deal with types, forms, qualities, or aspects of the speech subject.* You might discuss types of college students (freshman through seniors), breeds of show dogs (poodles through English bulldogs), qualities important for attaining some goal (being well educated), types of speeches (to entertain, inform, persuade), or types of birth control devices (pills, diaphragms, IUDs). Most subjects can be arranged topically in a variety of ways. You might, for example, talk about types of college students in terms of class standing, gender, major, or career objectives. Thus, the topical approach is quite flexible.

If you decide to arrange your speech topically, you concern yourself with two issues. First, you must select a topical scheme that allows you to deal comprehensively with your subject within a limited number of headings. If, for instance, you planned to discuss breeds of dogs, you would have to mention several dozen. Restricting yourself to breeds of show dogs would help—or even more specifically to breeds of small show dogs (define "small" early in the speech). Secondly, you should take a moment to tell your audience briefly why you have chosen this approach to your subject. Perhaps you are going to focus on small dogs because those are the ones with which you have had experience; maybe they are the most rare or the hardest to breed. Whatever your reasoning, share it with your audience so that they are not left wondering why you have limited yourself in such a way.

Causal Order

There are two methods of using the causal pattern of organization, moving either from cause to effect or from effect to cause. Audiences are often curious about why certain things have happened. Why are there too few students and too many schools in the community? Why are so few college students pursuing careers demanding a strong math background? Why are women experiencing an increase in cardiovascular disease? Why are so many American businesspeople concerned about Japanese competition? Whenever you are interested in answering these kinds of questions, you might want to organize your remarks using a causal sequence. If you and your audience are already aware that a problem exists (such as teenage pregnancies), you would not need to spend much time discussing the problem. Rather, you might briefly acknowledge the effect and go directly to the causes that seem to have contributed to it. With this speech, then, you might spend most of your time discussing the lack of sex education in homes and schools, the sexually permissive climate existing in our society, and the needs that some young women try to fulfill by getting pregnant.

A causal speech is always analytical. It can be either informative or persuasive. You might want to inform your classmates about the causes of teenage pregnancy as a general societal problem so that they better understand its complexity. Or, in contrast, you might decide that you want to convince a group of concerned parents that the absence of sex education is a primary cause of this problem. Depending on your purpose, you would treat the information differently, stressing different aspects and drawing different conclusions.

Ascending-Descending Order

If you select ascending-descending order as your pattern of organization, you first select some criterion for ordering your material. Then you arrange your information according to the amount of that criterion each point possesses. Suppose, for example, you use size as a criterion. You might then discuss models of Oldsmobiles moving from the largest to the smallest (descending) or vice versa (ascending). Or you might select importance as your criterion in examining the works of Shakespeare, moving from least to most important. Other topics that lend themselves well to either an ascending or a descending order include: Secrets of Effective Listening, Great Paintings of the Renaissance, Large Mountains in North America, Poisonous Snakes, and Great Political Leaders. In each of these examples you might easily organize your remarks by moving from the lesser to the greater or from the least important to the most important.

This pattern of organization can be used effectively with either informative or persuasive presentations. You would probably hope to gain the audience's understanding, for example, if you spoke about poisonous snakes. If you chose to speak about great American political leaders, however, you might want to convince the audience that those you selected were, in fact, significant. Moreover, you might want to convince them further that one particular American (e.g., Thomas Jefferson) was the greatest leader of all time.

In making a speech using either an ascending or a descending pattern of organization, you need to clarify your ordering criterion. This criterion creates a clear organizational framework for your presentation. The audience can then see how and why you have chosen to discuss your main ideas as you have. They might not always agree with your perceptions of importance or greatness, but at least they can follow your speech with relative ease.

Scientific Problem Solving Pattern

Many public speeches fall into a basic problem-solution format. One of the most thorough traditional approaches to developing a speech according to this method is the scientific problem solving pattern. Based on John Dewey's reflective thinking system(4), this pattern involves several systematic steps:

A. Define or describe the problem.
B. Analyze the causes and effects of the problem.
C. Examine alternative approaches to solving the problem, including strengths and weaknesses of each.
D. Select the preferred solution.

Some speakers insert another step into this sequence; that is, before examining alternatives they identify criteria that should be met by a good solution and then use those criteria to test the strength of each presented alternative.

This pattern of organization can represent an excellent approach to problem solving, depending upon the speaking situation. If you are confronted with a group of people who know almost nothing about the subject you are discussing, you might want to consider using this pattern of organization. It works well with uninformed audiences because it gives you the opportunity to provide fundamental information about the problem and its causes and effects before moving on to consider alternatives. Similarly, this pattern is advantageous with audiences who are hostile or opposed to the alternative you plan to advocate. As you examine the problem using this organizational strategy, you demonstrate to the audience your knowledge and your ability and willingness to consider the problem in an open-minded manner. Moreover, as you move through alternatives you demonstrate that you are, in fact, aware of different potential ways of dealing with the problem, again reinforcing your knowledge and open-mindedness. By the time you get around to your advocated solution, the audience should be willing to give you a real opportunity to present your case.

State-the-Case-and-Prove-It Order

An entirely different problem-solution order involves stating your position or case and then moving on to prove it. This approach is particularly useful with audiences who are already well aware of the existence of a problem. Neither do you have to convince them that a problem exists; nor do you have to explain to them the problem's causes and effects. Rather, your purpose with this kind of speech is to explain your reasons for favoring a particular plan or solution. The bulk of your speaking time is devoted to a discussion of how and why your position is sound or feasible.

In the introduction of a state-the-case-and-prove-it presentation, you usually acknowledge the fact that the audience is familiar with the problem. Then you explain your rationale for reopening a discussion of the issue. Perhaps new information has accumulated or recent events have modified a previously stable situation. Then you move on to each of your arguments along with supporting evidence. With a supportive, knowledgeable audience this pattern works very well.

Psychological-Progressive Pattern

A final problem-solution pattern of organization that is quite versatile is the psychological-progressive pattern. This organizational approach is appropriate with subjects that involve issues of feeling and emotion as well as fact and logic. (5). It involves these five steps:

A. Arouse
B. Dissatisfy
C. Gratify
D. Picture
E. Move

If you use this pattern of organization, you might begin with a moving story depicting the problem (for instance, an illustration of the effects of drug abuse, child pornography, or anorexia). Then you would go on to show the extent to which the problem is significant, possibly demonstrating its magnitude or complexity. Next you need to propose a solution, offer some hope, and reassure the audience that something can, in fact, be done. Next you specify how your solution might be brought to fruition and describe the extent to which the problem will diminish or even cease to exist. Finally, appeal to your audience to get involved, act, vote, or somehow commit themselves to your cause.

As you can see, this pattern of organization has the potential for being quite moving, if handled tastefully and ethically. The speaker using this pattern will use emotional appeals, but she must also present reasoned arguments to support her cause. Because this pattern allows one to picture vividly the effects of problems and to portray graphically both the problem and the solutions's positive effects, speakers often use it with "human interest" issues, such as child abuse, drunken driving, nuclear war, mercy killing, and capital punishment. The pattern can be used, however, with almost any topic that lends itself to a problem-solution format.

Transitions

Regardless of the pattern of organization you choose, you need to concern yourself with moving smoothly and logically from point to point. Even if you have constructed a well-organized speech, there is no guarantee that your audience will perceive that organization without some help. *That is, as you move from one major point to another, you need to provide excellent transitions, like bridges connecting one idea to the next.*

Sometimes transitions can be brief. You might say, for instance, "Now that we have examined some of the effects of this problem, let us move next to a consideration of its causes." *On other occasions you may need to write an entire paragraph to explain how or why you plan to proceed in a certain way.* Say, for example, that you are going to discuss the parking facilities problem at your college. You have articulated the nature of the problem, and now you want to go on to examine its causes. Before you do, however, you may need to discuss how the campus developed physically, since that is a major contributor to the present dilemma. In this case you would need to develop a good transition section, explaining to the audience why you need to examine historically the physical growth of the campus. Otherwise, the audience may perceive this information as an irrelevant tangent and simply tune you out.

Some speakers use rhetorical questions as transitions. Here are some examples: "But what do we really mean by the word 'educated'?" "If I asked you to, could you construct the profile of an ideal leader?" "What prevents people from learning new information?" "What are some of the barriers to effective communication?" These kinds of questions suggest the direction that you want the audience's thoughts to take.

If you use a preview as part of your speech's introduction, you may need only to say later in the speech, "first, second, and third" in moving from point to point. But you should not rely on this method of transition for every speech.

Internal summaries can also be used as transitions. If you are dealing with an especially complex subject, you may want to summarize briefly what you have just said before going on to the next point. You might say, for example, "At this point we have briefly examined four major barriers that tend to prevent students from learning. We've looked at fear, mindset, cognitive impairment, and lack of discipline. Clearly, there are no ready solutions to such complex and diversified problems. But there *are* some approaches that have been tried at several experimental learning centers on the East Coast. Some have been quite successful. In the moments that remain I'd like to share with you some of these findings as possible ways to address these difficult problems." However, you would not use this type of internal summary very often and never with simple, straightforward topics for fear of insulting the audience's intelligence or being redundant.

Good transitions are important. Without them the audience may not see the unity of your presentation or grasp the interrelatedness of your ideas. They may not learn or be persuaded. Through meaningful transitions you can reveal your organizational approach, show the audience how you think, and suggest to them the way they might be led to think. Good transitions are not merely a nice finishing touch; they are the bonds that unite your ideas and give them coherence.

OUTLINING

Most of the speeches you make will be delivered from an outline. Even on those occasions when you decide to make a formal manuscript presentation, you will still create outlines along the way to help you organize your thoughts and examine the structure of your speech. *Thus, outlining is a process you will use to help discover appropriate ways of arranging information and ideas.* As you begin to work on your speech and develop a purpose statement, you may jot down a rough outline that seems like a reasonable organizational approach. Later, as you conduct research and become better informed, some of your ideas may change. As your perspective is altered and your information pool enlarges, your outline will change too. When you are satisfied with the research and thinking you have done, you will need to create a final outline to be used during the actual delivery of your speech. In constructing the final outline, several guidelines may prove valuable.

First, *each point in your outline should contain only one idea or piece of information.* Here is a poor example:

I.   Excessive salt in the diet leads to water retention and has also been linked with high blood pressure and depression.

The above example is poor because it contains several different points. The following is an improved version:

I.   Salt should be minimized in the diet.

    A.   Excessive salt intake leads to water retention.
    B.   High blood pressure and excessive salt intake have been linked.
    C.   Depression is often associated with the use of excessive salt.

Notice how the main idea is presented with a Roman numeral. Each subpoint is identified with subordinate capital letters.

Second, *your outline should accurately reflect relationships between ideas.* The most basic, general ideas should be listed with Roman numerals, the next with capital letters, the next with Arabic numbers, and so on. Consider this poor example:

I.   Too much salt leads to high blood pressure.

    A.   Excessive salt intake causes water retention.
    B.   Depression and excessive salt use have been linked.
    C.   Salt substitutes should be explored.
    D.   Salt should be minimized in the diet.

The most general idea in this illustration is that salt should be minimized in the diet. Yet, that point has been made subordinate to the one claiming that salt leads to high blood pressure. In fact, none of the subpoints is related directly to the main point (I.). Here is a better approach to this outline:

I.   Salt should be minimized in the diet.

    A.   Diets containing too much salt produce several negative effects.

        1.   Adults often develop high blood pressure.
        2.   All age groups tend to become obese.
        3.   Adults, especially women, tend to become depressed.

    B.   Minimizing salt in the diet does not mean that food must taste "flat."

        1.   Several good salt substitutes exist.
        2.   Other herbs and spices can be substituted for salt.

In this outline segment, one general idea is introduced with a Roman numeral. That main idea is developed by two slightly less general subpoints appearing under A and B. These, in turn, are elaborated through more specific subpoints appearing in 1, 2, and 3.

The example just presented illustrates another important outlining rule: *Each subpoint should be logically related to the main point under which it falls.* In the poor example that rule was consistently violated. Depression, for example, has nothing to do with high blood pressure. In the improved outline, however, each subpoint related logically to the main idea that salt should be minimized in the diet.

It is also important to *be consistent in the kind of phraseology you use.* You may choose to use a full sentence outline, such as the ones we have used above. Or you may prefer a topical or key word outlining approach. Here is a short example of a *key word* outline:

    I. Reasons to get an education

        A. Being an informed citizen
        B. Increasing one's social conscience
        C. Getting a better job
        D. Increasing one's income

   II. Kinds of college majors that are most promising

        A. Engineering
        B. Math
        C. Computer science
        D. Economics

Outlines should not jump back and forth between phrases and sentences. If you choose a sentence outline, keep the sentences reasonably concise to help you deliver your speech in a spontaneous, conversational manner.

Finally, *you should use a consistent system of symbols and indentation.* All main points should be listed with Roman numerals; all major subpoints should have capital letters; all supporting statements should have Arabic numbers. In short, follow the system illustrated below.

Purpose Statement: _____

Introduction

    I. Attention-getting device

   II. Orientation phase

        A. Key definitions
        B. Background
        C. Preview

Body

III. First main idea

    A. First main subpoint

        1. Support for this subpoint
           a. First piece of specific information
           b. Second piece of specific information
        2. More support for the first subpoint

    B. Second main subpoint

        1. First supporting statement
        2. Second supporting statement
           a. Specific information
           b. More specific information
               (1) Very detailed support
               (2) More detailed support
           c. More specific information

    C. Third main subpoint

        1. First supporting statement
        2. Second supporting statement

IV. Second main idea

    A. First main subpoint

    B. Second main subpoint

        1. First supporting statement
           a. Specific information
           b. More specific information
        2. Second supporting statement

V. Third main idea

Conclusion

VI. Summary

VII. Challenge

VIII. Quotation

This sample represents an abbreviated version of the kind of outline you will develop. Perhaps you will change it in certain ways. You may, for example, want to write out your introduction and conclusion. Or you may choose to write out transitions so that you move smoothly from point to point. You may also decide to fill in certain supporting details, such as expert testimony or statistics. Thus, this illustration represents only an example to be used with flexibility.

Unfortunately, the outlining guidelines presented here are often violated, although they are not difficult to master. A carefully constructed outline is of great help during the delivery of any speech. Just as important, it stands as tangible evidence of the time, effort, and thought you have put into your speech.

INTRODUCING YOUR SPEECH

The patterns of arrangement we discussed earlier in this chapter represent different ways you might choose to organize the main ideas in your speech. These main points, or the *body* of your speech, must be introduced in some way. Although there are many different kinds of speech introductions, each should do two things: *catch the audience's attention* and *provide some audience orientation.* Audiences assemble for public speeches with many things on their minds. Some audience members have had stressful days. Others are preoccupied with responsibilities they have after the speech is over. Your classroom audience will have come from all over campus; they may be tired, frustrated, or excited about the course they just attended. That's why it is so important for you to spend some time at the beginning of your speech gaining their attention, making them want to listen, and providing a smooth transition into the body of your speech.

Many different attention-getting devices exist. Some work better with certain kinds of audiences or topics than with others. Humor, for example, usually works best with topics that are not overly somber, technical, or discouraging. The speaker who uses humor to introduce his speech on the effects of nuclear war would be, at the very least, using poor taste. Humor also works best when the speaker knows the audience very well so that she can predict the kinds of subjects they might find humorous. Thus, the best attention-gaining device will vary with the demands of the particular situation. Following, however, are some traditionally accepted, often effective, introductory devices.

Some speakers like to begin their speeches with a story or an illustration that leads into the topic. The story might be intriguing, humorous, emotional, or perplexing—but it must be interesting to be successful. An introductory story could be real or hypothetical. It might be personal in the sense of revealing something about your own life or experiences or it might deal with other people's lives or with something you have read. Following is one example of how Peggy Dersch, a student at Southeast Missouri State University, introduced her speech on rape in the Interstate Oratorical Association's annual contest:

> It was winter, 1976. A news item concerning the attempted rape of an eight-year-old child was reported on WABC-TV in New York City. Following the news, the station's weather announcer, Tex Antoine, began his report by reminding viewers of what he called an ancient proverb. "Confucious once say: If rape is inevitable, relax and enjoy it!" After enough protest calls, station officials required Antoine to offer a public apology. He said simply, "I regret making the statement." And then he added, "I didn't realize the victim was a child."(6)

The speaker then goes on to discuss the widespread ignorance concerning rape and urges the audience to think more critically about how they view this crime.

Another attention-getting introductory device is paying the audience a deserved compliment. Notice the word "deserved." This technique should be used only in circumstances where the speaker can extend congratulations or offer compliments with honesty. For example, when Karl D. Bays, chairman of the American Hospital Supply Corporation, spoke to students at the J. L. Kellogg Graduate School of Management at Northwestern University, he was well aware of their high caliber. Thus, he introduced his speech by saying:

> I'm delighted at the opportunity to meet this talented and accomplished group of people. It's a chance to add my congratulations to every one of you. Acceptance to this excellent school is a milestone in itself, and a significant step in your management careers.(7)

If you will stop and think for a moment of how attentive you are when someone tells you that you are intelligent, accomplished, or have made some significant achievement, you can see how potentially valuable this kind of introductory device can be.

In some speaking situations you may find that you and the audience have something in common. Perhaps you think it is an important commonality, like similar values, backgrounds, or problems. Yet, your audience may be unaware of it. *Since one of the best ways to establish rapport with any audience is to demonstrate what you have in common with them, using the introduction as an opportunity to establish common ground is a excellent attention-gaining device.* In the example that follows, Milan Nastich, president of Ontario Hydro, began his speech to a large group of Canadian engineering students in this way:

> When Neil Payne extended the invitation to speak to you today, he pointed out that I would be speaking to a student audience. I remembered that students sometimes have the reputation for being difficult audiences—critical, volatile, and highly vocal.
>
> But then I remembered that you would be engineers, a breed apart from other students—courteous, serious, no-nonsense, high-minded individuals dedicated to the betterment of mankind, and not inclined to indulge in the frivolities that distract so many non-engineering types. I can say this from experience. I was an engineering student myself just a couple of decades ago.(8)

Actually, this introduction uses three devices: paying the audience a compliment, establishing common ground, and humor. Many good speakers do create introductions with more than one of these devices, providing a broader potential for gaining the audience's attention.

Another attention-getting technique appropriate with some topics is the use of an intriguing or startling statement or series of statements. By peaking the audience's curiosity these statements are often quite helpful in gaining their attention. In the following example, Kathy Weisensel, a junior at the University of Wisconsin, used this intriguing introduction in her basic speech class.

> There is a problem which is shared by millions of people in the United States. It knows no barrier to age, sex, or social class. Yet, it is a problem that for years

was hidden in society's darkest closet. Only recently has the closet door begun to open. That problem is mental retardation.(9).

In reading this brief introduction you may find yourself wondering at first what she is going to address—perhaps venereal disease, incest, or even suicide. As you wonder, you become actively involved in the communication process, eager to listen and learn. Thus, your attention belongs to the speaker.

On occasion, you may be discussing a subject of such great interest or significance that the most appropriate introduction is to go directly to the purpose of your talk. This is especially fitting if the audience members are aware of your subject in advance, are already motivated to want to learn about it, and view the subject as serious. In this context a "let's get on with it" approach is usually best. In the introduction that follows, Ivan Hill, president emeritus of the Ethics Resource Center, began his speech to the Associated General Contractors in Houston with these initial remarks:

> I am here to discuss ethics. I have chosen the special topic "Compromise and Conviction" because these factors constitute a continuously recurrent ethical dilemma.(10)

Then he goes on to distinguish his view of ethics from those of others. With this kind of introduction the speaker can reassure the audience that he is not going to waste their time, but will move directly to the point of the presentation.

A final introductory device is *humor.* Although if used properly humor can be one of the best attention-getting devices, it can also have disastrous consequences if used unwisely. Nothing could be more humiliating than telling a joke at the beginning of your speech only to have the audience remain politely silent. *Humor usually works best in the situation where the speaker knows the audience well. Above all, a humorous introduction should be relevant to the subject of the speech.* No matter how hilarious a joke you heard in your fraternity house last Friday night, resist the temptation to tell it at the beginning of your speech unless it is clearly relevant. Dean Bruce Lockerbie, dean of the faculty at the Stony Brook School, used humor in addressing his audience of students and teachers:

> There's a story about a chicken and a pig who were passing a church, when they noticed the signboard and its weekly message: "What have you given to God today?" The chicken looked at the pig, the pig looked at the chicken, and each agreed that it had been a long time since either one of them had given God anything.
>
> "Pig," said the chicken, "I think we ought to mend our ways."
>
> "I agree," said the pig. "What exactly do you have in mind?"
>
> The chicken thought for a moment, then said, "Pig, you and I ought to give God a plate of ham-and-eggs."
>
> "You can't be serious!" replied the pig.
>
> "Why not?" said the chicken, offended that his suggestion had been rebuffed. "Don't you think God would be pleased by our token offering?"

"That's just the point," the pig retorted. "What for you may be a token offering, for me is total commitment!"(11)

The speaker continues, discussing the need for people who are totally committed to the educational process. Thus, this humorous story is clearly relevant.

Besides getting the audience's attention, the other major function of the introduction is to *orient the audience.* Some speakers make the mistake of tossing out a jazzy attention-getter and then jumping directly into the body of the speech. For most audiences, such practices are jarring. *What is needed is a way to move gracefully from the initial attention-getter to the main points of the speech. We call this "way of getting there" the audience orientation phase of the introduction.* What should be included in this part of the introduction will vary with the topic, audience, and situation, but it is quite common for an orientation phase to include all or some of the following: a *definition of terms,* a *purpose statement, background information,* and a *preview* of points to come.

If, for example, you were going to use a new word, discuss a controversial issue, or deal with a particular aspect of a subject, you might want to make your intention clear through a direct definition of terms. You might say, "When I talk about compensation for the handicapped, I am referring to those who have physical handicaps, such as multiple sclerosis, blindness, or deafness. I am excluding all learning disabilities and mental retardation." In this manner you can avoid much subsequent confusion. Another way you can prepare the audience for your remarks is to provide a direct, clear statement of purpose. You could say, "What I want to do tonight is convince you to join the union." Or suppose you were going to deal with a complex problem. Perhaps you have decided that your purpose is only to discuss the causes and effects of the problem; that is, you think it might be premature to advocate a solution, or maybe you're not yet certain of the preferred solution. In order to clarify your intent and suggest appropriate audience expectations, you should state the fact that you plan only to discuss the problem and that such analysis will indeed be the major thrust of your speech. Without a purpose statement to clarify your plan, some listeners may be impatient to hear you move to the solution or may wonder how long your speech is going to be since you are discussing the problem at such a leisurely pace.

You can also use the orientation phase to give background for your topic. If you are going to discuss contemporary trends in advertising, for example, you might want first to give a brief historical overview in order to acclimate the audience to the context out of which contemporary trends grew. Finally, you may want to preview or present an overview of the points you plan to cover. Previewing is another method of clarifying the procedure you plan to pursue. While the purpose statement states your goal, the preview mentions your method. Previews are especially useful when you are trying to be instructive or when you feel a special need to clarify your intentions. Together, these orientation devices provide an extended transition from the attention-getter into the body of the speech. They prepare the audience by specifying speaker goals, methods, and definitions, and provide background on the subject to be discussed.

CONCLUDING YOUR SPEECH

Many public speakers do not conclude their speeches—they simply stop talking. Or they stammer through their concluding remarks in such a way that they nearly ruin the effectiveness of their presentation. Your speech's conclusion is very important. If you work to construct it carefully, your conclusion can serve to round out your speech and being it to a strategic close. Because it is the last part of your speech, the audience will remember it more clearly than they will information appearing in the middle of your presentation.(12) Thus, you have a real opportunity to create a final positive impact.

There are many ways to conclude speeches. One common technique is the *summary.* Summaries are particularly useful with speeches that are complex or rather long. *The summary serves to reinforce the ideas presented and remind the audience of the speech's most important points.* In the example that follows, John R. Bonee, corporate manager of Illinois Bell, concluded his speech to the National Conference of the Public Relations Students Society of America with this summary:

> I've talked about the theoretical barriers and the practical problems you face in managing your relationship with your speaker. They are: Prejudice in favor of overwhelming people with everything you know about the subject, the assumption that you always need to write for the eye instead of the ear. On the practical side, I talked about the problems you run into because of people between you and the speaker, the problem of clearances by subject matter experts, and the problem of merchandising what the boss has said.
>
> This has not been a "how to" presentation. I haven't given you a bunch of rules of thumb, 1-2-3-4-5, and if you follow them you'll be a great speech writer. I've given you just a few age-old principles of effective oratory.(13)

Most of the time summaries do not stand alone. Often, they are or should be accompanied by some other, more compelling concluding device. In the conclusion that follows, for example, Karl D. Bays ended his speech with a brief summary followed by a *challenge:*

> I hope you'll remember some more ancient values that apply just as effectively to the work of management. I'm talking about the values of hard work, creativity, self-fulfillment and service to other people.
>
> Those may be older values than the latest organizational methods and marketing theories. But they're old because they work. They apply to the job of management and to the jobs of the people you'll manage in the future. They're values that can help us, as managers, in improving productivity.
>
> The world needs your skills, your abilities and your productivity. It needs your zest and curiosity, your courage and generosity. And I feel that you, as managers, have an opportunity to deliver all that, and more.
>
> I'm an eternal optimist about the progress that we, as managers, can create. And I'm so glad you're planning to take part. I wish you all the best of luck.(14)

Another potentially compelling concluding devide is the quotation. Quotations can be taken from poetry, plays, songs, speeches, or from other great literature. Some of the most moving quotations come from people whose names are familiar to us. Bonita L. Perry, a communicator psychologist with the Sun Company, used a persuasive quotation in closing her speech on building successful careers to the American Women in Radio and TV. Perry said:

> In closing, I suggest that we weave into our career perspectives these words from the courageous Helen Keller. She said: "Security is mostly a superstition. It does not exist in nature, nor do the children of men as a whole experience it. Avoiding danger is no safer in the long run than outright exposure. Life is either a daring adventure or nothing."
>
> I suggest that choosing between those two outcomes—a "daring adventure" or "nothing"—is not a difficult choice.(15)

Still another concluding device often used to end persuasive speeches is the appeal. Appeals may be either logical or emotional. They usually make some attempt to move the audience, to act or believe or feel more strongly about the speaker's proposition. In his speech to the nation on Cambodia, April 30, 1970, President Richard M. Nixon concluded with this appeal:

> It is customary to conclude a speech from the White House by asking support for the President of the United States.
>
> Tonight, I depart from that precedent. What I ask is far more important. I ask for your support for our brave men fighting tonight halfway around the world, not for territory, not for glory, but so that their younger brothers and their sons and your sons can have a chance to grow up in a world of peace and freedom, and justice.(16)

Finally, you may choose to conclude your speech by visualizing the future. This technique is particularly appropriate if you are giving a speech in which you advocate some change that would make the academic community, the state, or even the world a different, hopefully better, place. The late Dr. Martin Luther King, Jr. used this concluding device effectively in his speech at the 1963 civil rights march:

> When we allow freedom to ring, when we let it ring from every village and every hamlet, from every state and every city, we will be able to speed up that day when all of God's children, black men and white men, Jews and Gentiles, Protestants and Catholics, will be able to join hands and sing in the words of the old Negro spiritual, "Free at last! Free at last! Thank God Almighty, we are free at last!"(17)

Conclusions, like introductions, will vary according to the demands of the speaking situation, your topic, and the audience. In general, however, they should be relatively brief. Audiences usually find it very annoying when a speaker says,

"Finally," and then drones on for another fifteen minutes. When you say, "In conclusion," immediately follow through with a concise, carefully planned conclusion that reinforces your purpose and creates a final positive impact.

A SUMMARIZING NOTE

Presenting a well-organized speech is important. Excellent ideas can be lost in a poorly organized, muddled presentation. Even a sparkling delivery cannot compensate for disorganization. Think for a moment of how you react when you hear a speaker who seems disorganized. Do you tend to label the person unprepared? Careless? Scatterbrained? Maybe even dumb? Are you willing to continue listening to a speaker who cannot "get his act together" and present a cogent, well-organized speech? Probably not! Given the listening difficulties we discussed earlier in this book, it seems clear that the disorganized speaker gives the listening audience every excuse to tune her out.

In contrast, a well-organized presentation suggests certain things about the speaker—intelligence, conscientiousness, the ability to think logically, and concern for listeners. Any speaker who is perceived in those kinds of terms is bound to benefit from such a highly credible image. Of course, there's no guarantee that being well organized will assure the positive acceptance of your ideas. The chances are good, however, that the audience will be able to learn from you, respect you, and follow your persuasive point. And those accomplishments alone are significant. Thus, sound organization establishes a framework in which your speaking objectives are likely to be achieved.

EXERCISES

1. Read the first speech that appears in the Appendix. Then do the following:

    a. Identify the introductory device used. Is it effective?

    b. What pattern of organization is the speaker using? Do you see any points at which the speech is not as clearly organized as it might be? How could it be improved?

    c. Outline the body of the speech following the rules of outlining presented in this chapter.

    d. To what extent did the speaker effectively use transitions? Write down three or more transitions that the speaker used.

    e. Identify the concluding device used and comment on its appropriateness.

2. Select a topic for a speech. After you have selected your purpose, narrowed it appropriately, and conducted some preliminary thinking and research, prepare a rough outline. During the next few days continue to think and do research. After you feel you are ready to reconsider your initial approach to the topic, go back to the rough outline. Rework it and begin to refine it. Write out the introduction and conclusion. Also write out your transitions. Make sure you follow the rules for outlining presented in this chapter. Now you are ready to think about the delivery of your speech.

3. As you listen to others deliver their speeches, pay particular attention to the patterns of organization they have chosen. See if you can identify them and then ask yourself

•

how you would have organized the same subject if you were discussing it with an audience. What might account for some of the differences you discover?

4. As you listen to other speakers, try to identify three or four common problems with organization. List and share them with other listeners, with the goal of seeking possible remedies.

NOTES

1. John E. Baird, Jr., "The Effects of 'Previews' and 'Reviews' Upon Audience Comprehension of Expository Speeches of Varying Quality and Complexity," *Central States Speech Journal* 25 (1974), pp. 119–127; Ernest Thompson, "An Experimental Investigation of the Relative Effectiveness of Organizational Structures in Oral Communication," *Southern Speech Journal* 26 (1960), pp. 59–69.

2. Harry Sharp and Thomas McClung, "Effects of Organization of the Speaker's Ethos," *Speech Monographs* 33 (1966), pp. 182–183.

3. Baird, pp. 119–127.

4. John Dewey, *How We Think* (Boston: Heath, 1910).

5. The psychological progressive pattern is based on Monroe's Motivated Sequence; see Alan H. Monroe and Douglas Ehninger, *Principles and Types of Speeches* (Glenview, Ill.: Scott, Foresman & Co., 1967), pp. 264–289.

6. Peggy Dersch, "Do You Think You Know Me?" in *Contemporary American Speeches,* 5th ed., eds. W. A. Linkugel and others (Dubuque, Iowa: Kendall/Hunt, 1978), p. 232.

7. Karl D. Bays, "Perspectives on Productivity: Let's Not Forget the Managers," *Vital Speeches of the Day* 48 (Oct. 15, 1981), p. 25.

8. Milan Nastich, "Technology, Engineering, and the Environment," *Vital Speeches of the Day* 48 (Feb. 15, 1982), p. 298.

9. Kathy Weisensel, "David: And A Whole Lot of Other Neat People," in *Contemporary American Speeches,* 5th ed., eds. W. A. Linkugel and others (Dubuque, Iowa: Kendall/Hunt, 1978), p. 80.

10. Ivan Hill, "Compromise and Conviction: The Ethical Dilemma," *Vital Speeches of the Day* 48 (May 1, 1982), p. 434.

11. D. Bruce Lockerbie, "Teaching Who We Are," *Vital Speeches of the Day* 48 (May 15, 1982), p. 476.

12. The research dealing with whether or not individuals better remember information presented first (primacy) or last (recency) is mixed. Scholars agree, however, that both are better remembered than information presented in the middle. See, for example, E. E. Jones and G. R. Goethals, *Attribution: Perceiving the Causes of Behavior* (Morristown, New Jersey: General Learning Press, 1972), pp. 27–46.

13. John R. Bonee, "The Care and Feeding of the Executive Speaker," *Vital Speeches of the Day* 48 (Jan. 15, 1982), p. 202.

14. Bays, p. 27.

15. Bonita L. Perry, "Three Career Traps for Women," *Vital Speeches of the Day* 48 (Nov. 15, 1981), p. 79.

16. Richard M. Nixon, "Cambodia," in *Contemporary American Speeches,* 5th ed., eds. W. A. Linkugel and others (Dubuque, Iowa: Kendall/Hunt, 1978), p. 318–319.

17. Martin Luther King, Jr., "I Have A Dream," in *Contemporary American Speeches,* 5th ed., eds. W. A. Linkugel and others (Dubuque, Iowa: Kendall/Hunt, 1978), p. 370.

chapter 9

Presenting the Speech

CHAPTER OBJECTIVES

After studying this chapter you should be able to:

1. Compare and contrast different types of speech delivery.
2. Recall basic principles of effective delivery.
3. List the characteristics of good oral style.
4. Construct visual aids that reinforce your speech.
5. Deliver a speech effectively.
6. Conduct an audience question/answer session using the principles outlined in this chapter.

INTRODUCTION

You are really excited. You are sitting in an audience about to listen to a speaker you have admired for years. Having studied computer science in college, you want very much to pursue a career using your skills and knowledge. The woman who is about to address you is vice president of one of the largest computer manufacturers in the country; thus, she has a great deal of credibility in your eyes.

After she is introduced, your would-be role model rises and begins to speak. You, however, can hardly believe what you are seeing and hearing. She stands rigidly behind the podium, grasping it with both hands, her knuckles turning white. She never looks up during the entire presentation of her speech. Instead, she reads her manuscript line by line. She never moves, never gestures, and speaks in a soft, flat voice, droning on and on. Beside feeling relieved when she is finished, you also start to wonder how in the world this woman ever got to be a vice president. Certainly not on the basis of her public speaking ability!

As you can see, a public speaker's presentational skills are extremely important. Many audience members know little about sound evidence or reasoning. They may be rather fuzzy on the subject of organization. But they can *all* recognize poor delivery when they see it. Even the most ignorant or untutored audience member notices poor eye contact, awkward gestures, or a monotone voice. Moreover, he or she will make judgments about the speaker's trustworthiness and competence on the basis of vocal characteristics and other delivery qualities.

Perhaps it is unfair for a speaker who has labored for days to prepare a speech that is well researched, filled with excellent evidence, and effectively organized to be judged so harshly if her presentational skills are lacking. But even if we acknowledge this apparent lack of justice, we must also be realistic in recognizing that audience's do react strongly to the presentational quality of any speech. Unfortunately, sometimes they weigh delivery skills so heavily that a speaker with poor content but a sterling delivery may receive a very high rating. Thus, it is crucial that you develop effective presentational skills. Without them, all the rest of your speech preparation efforts may be in vain. Presentational skills include using your voice, body, language, and visual aids as effectively as possible.

TYPES OF DELIVERY

When you are ready to consider the actual delivery of your speech, you need to begin by deciding the general style or type of delivery you want to use. *Most speakers need to develop the ability to use different delivery styles since different occasions and topics call for or suggest different approaches.* You would not want to speak to a large, formal meeting with a casual, off-the-cuff style, nor would you want to speak to your classmates about the need to support the football team by writing out and reading a manuscript to them. *What is important, then, is to fit the delivery style to the situation in which you find yourself. Finally, whatever your presentational preferences, your delivery should never call attention to itself.* If members of your audience walk away from your presentation commenting on your marvelous gestures or the way you used your voice to emphasize key points, chances are that your delivery actually distracted them from the ideas you were discussing. Your presentational style, then, should reinforce your remarks rather than compete with them for attention.

One popular delivery style is *impromptu.* Impromptu speaking is off-the-cuff and causal, delivered with little or no time for preparation or practice. Generally, you should never choose to make an impromptu speech if you have time to prepare in advance. However, you may be sitting in a business meeting one evening and the chairperson may ask you to comment spontaneously on an issue or report on a conference you have just attended. In such a situation you have little choice but to make impromptu remarks.

Speech teachers often use "rounds of impromptus" early in the semester to give everyone a chance to stand in front of the class and talk. Impromptus can be creative and enjoyable in this context, especially if approached with good humor and good will. With this kind of presentation you can still use basic principles of good organization, sound evidence and reasoning, and direct, fluent delivery. Good delivery will be more difficult under these circumstances, however.

Another mode of delivery, representing the other extreme of the formality continuum, is *manuscript speaking*. If you choose to make this kind of speech, you need to write out your speech word for word and read it from the manuscript. There are many problems commonly associated with manuscript speaking. Some manuscript speakers never look up, their eyes remaining glued to the script. Others sound as if they are reading an article from the newspaper rather than sharing their own ideas. Still others lapse into a monotone. Many remain hidden behind the podium, using few gestures and no bodily movement. Thus, it is easy to lose directness and spontaneity when speaking from a manuscript.

In spite of the problems just mentioned, manuscript speaking is very common. Many political and business leaders feel compelled to use manuscripts because they must have precise records of what they have said in order to avoid being misquoted by the press. Still others use a manuscript as a way of acknowledging the importance and formality of the speaking occasion. These speakers use manuscripts so that they can take great pains with their language and their transitions, and make sure they stay well within the time limits. They view the manuscript as a method for maintaining control over their presentation.

If you decide to use a manuscript, do so for the right reasons. Use a manuscript to enhance the care with which you present your remarks. Use it to control time and to allow you to select interesting, colorful language. Then prepare to practice it over and over again. You must become familiar with the manuscript so that you can look away from it and establish eye contact with your audience. Your manuscript is not intended to be a straightjacket. It can be changed. Different examples can be added. Spontaneous comments can (and should) be included. Small portions of it can be committed to memory so that you can feel free to gesture and move occasionally. Under these conditions manuscript delivery can be quite compelling.

The final style of delivery, the one that is appropriate for most speaking occasions, is *extemporaneous*. When you speak extemporaneously, you will probably have your key points fixed in your mind, but each time you deliver the speech you will vary the use of examples, precise words, and phrases. Extemporaneous speaking is *not* the same as impromptu, though the two are often confused. Extemporaneous speaking demands a careful, thorough preparation process.

Most extemporaneous speeches are delivered from outlines like the ones discussed in the preceding chapter. Some speakers like to put their outlines onto note cards so that they are free to carry them around and move from behind the podium. Others prefer to have their outlines on two or three full sheets of paper so that they can see where they are going without having to turn to the next card. The real advantages of extemporaneous delivery are spontaneity and directness. The extemporaneous speaker is one who should be able to make eye contact with the audience, watch for audience reactions, move and gesture freely, and speak conversationally. His outline permits flexibility and sensitivity to the demands of the situation.

Of course, extemporaneous speaking has its pitfalls too. Without the security of being armed with a manuscript, the speaker may lose his place, go blank, or flounder for words. However, with appropriate preliminary practice the speech should go smoothly. Moreover, since this form of delivery is much like enlarged conversation, it is not likely to call attention to itself.

DELIVERY: SOME GUIDING PRINCIPLES

Regardless of the style of delivery you choose, you should approach the presentation of your speech with some fundamental guiding principles. Because principles are not the same as rules, they can be applied with flexibility. You should *adjust your style of delivery to the demands of the speaking situation.* Should you use a podium? Should you gesture during your speech? How about walking or moving about occasionally? How quickly should you talk? Will vocal projection be a problem? Is it ever appropriate to sit down while making a speech? There are no absolute responses to any of these questions. The answers depend on many things. What is appropriate in one situation may be tasteless in another. The speaker who pulls up a chair and sits down in front of an auditorium packed with several hundred people is ignoring the formality of the setting. However, the speaker who stands stiffly behind a massive podium and reads a manuscript to a small group of five or six people is equally ignorant of appropriate informality. That's why the principles that follow should be used flexibly.

Establish Eye Contact

Have you ever talked to anyone who had difficulty looking you in the eye? How did you react? Did you feel that the person was uncomfortable? Nervous? Ashamed? Preoccupied? Dishonest? When a communicator cannot look us in the eye we often respond negatively. The same is true in public speaking situations. Our eyes are very expressive. As we squint, smile, laugh, frown, and scowl we communicate many emotions. We demonstrate our concern, our commitment, our anger, or our joy. *The speaker who fails to establish eye contact must rely on his voice, his words, and other bodily movements to convey these feelings.* Thus, he is handicapped.

Another reason for establishing eye contact with audience members is to establish credibility. We are more likely to believe a speaker who looks us in the eye while defending his point of view. Because he can look at us while talking about his subject, he shows us that he is well versed rather than buried in his notes. Moreover, we tend to believe (although not always with justification) that anyone who looks us in the eye while making a point is unlikely to mislead us. Thus, establishing eye contact is a way of demonstrating honesty, sincerity, and trustworthiness.

Finally, by establishing eye contact you have a chance to watch the audience's reactions. How can you see those yawns or glazed expressions if you never look

Students in a informal setting speak with more spontaneity and more directness than they do when in a formal gathering. They gesture freely, use various facial expressions, and deliver their words in a conversational manner. (Photo courtesy of John Lei, Omni Photo Communications, Inc.)

up? Equally important, how will you benefit from appreciative smiles and nods of encouragement? You cannot be responsive to audience feedback if you don't see it. Almost all audience feedback will be nonverbal until after the speech is over. Thus, by "closing your eyes" you miss out on the chance to adjust to audience reactions.

As you strive to establish good eye contact with your audience, remember to share your attention with everyone. Avoid focusing on only a few people (perhaps your friends) or glancing only at the front, the back, the right, or the left side of the room. Also avoid darting eyes, glancing up and down from the outline as if bobbing for apples, or staring at any member of the audience as if in a trance. Of all the principles of effective delivery, this one is probably the most global. *It is hard to imagine a communication situation where good eye contact would fail to be an asset.*

Reinforce with Gestures, Movements, and Facial Expressions

Most of us use numerous gestures in daily conversation. We talk with our hands, point, wave our fists, and pound on the table to stress a point. We also move around. We pace, slouch in our chairs, move closer to convey liking or intimacy, or move further away to create distance or convey aloofness. We communicate a great deal with our faces too. We smile broadly, scowl, raise an eyebrow, or stick out our lower lip and clench our teeth to convey determination or stubborness. Interestingly, however, the person who is quite animated in daily discourse may become rigid and immobile when making a speech. The act of standing before others makes many speakers uncomfortable. Suddenly they don't know what to do with their hands, their feet, or their bodies. So they do nothing—they stand lifelessly behind the podium. Only their head moves from time to time, but the arms and hands are never seen, and their face remains expressionless. Other speakers react differently. In a seeming fit of super-energy, they move around the front of the room, eyes glowing wildly, continuously pacing back and forth, and punching the air with sharp, repetitive gestures.

Clearly, such extremes are to be avoided. *Taken together, your movements, gestures, and facial expressions should reinforce the points you are making.* Through gestures, for example, you can accent an idea, demonstrate a relationship, depict contrast, and so forth. Suppose you are comparing the experience of attending one of the "big-ten" universities with that of attending a small, private liberal arts college. As you move from one kind of school to the other in the actual content of your speech, you might move smoothly from behind the podium to one side of it. In this instance your movement serves as a transition, showing the audience that you are moving from one major idea to another. At the same time, you are demonstrating contrast. You could do the same thing by extending first your right and then your left hand in discussing each type of school respectively. Thus, different kinds of gestures and movements can be used to make the same point.

What is important here is that your words and your actions be mutually reinforcing. If you were talking with a friend about something that really matters to you and you said, "I *really* want you to do this," you would lean forward, peer straight into her eyes, and nod your head emphatically. All of your actions and expressions would accent your persuasive point. Yet, many speakers make the same comment to audiences with a deadpan face, little eye contact, and no gestures or movement. No audience is going to be moved by such a bland and contradictory appeal!

Perhaps you are uncertain if your movements, gestures, and facial expressions are appropriate. In this instance you need to watch yourself speak in front of a mirror or ask someone to listen to you and give you feedback. Among the questions you might pose are these:

1. Do I gesture enough? Too much?
2. Does my movement seem to reinforce the flow of the speech?
3. Are any of my gestures distracting?
4. Do I rely too much on any one gesture?
5. Does my face convey the meaning I am trying to get across?
6. Are there different gestures, movements, or facial expressions that might convey my intended meaning more effectively?

Although some basic movements and gestures can be planned and rehearsed in advance, most should occur spontaneously as you speak. Thus, your movements would vary as you give the same speech on different occasions. For instance, natural conversational gestures would work quite well with audiences numbering 25 and under. But if you were speaking to 140 people in a church or an auditorium, you would need to enlarge your gestures, exaggerating them so that they can be seen by everyone.

Finally, even if you feel you cannot gesture very much or very often, make sure that your chosen movements are not nervous or distracting. Some speakers pace nervously. Others play with their earrings, stroke their hair, chew gum, or tap a pencil they forgot to leave behind. Still others use such exaggerated gestures that they look foolish and melodramatic. *In general, whenever a gesture calls attention to itself, eliminate it.*

Strive for an Effective Speaking Voice

Have you ever listened to a speaker whose voice drove you crazy? Perhaps she spoke in a monotone, stumbled over her words, or inserted "you know" between every other sentence. Or maybe her pitch was especially high, her pace breathlessly rapid, or her volume excessively loud. Clearly, our voices can get us into a lot of trouble as public speakers. But our voices can also be used fully and compellingly to convey our intended meaning. *When we use our voices effectively we can emphasize key ideas, display a wide variety of emotions, and enhance our own credibility.*

In examining your own speaking voice you might begin by speaking into a tape recorder and playing it back several times. Once again, obtaining feedback from friends could also be helpful since they are likely to notice peculiarities that might sound "normal" to you because you use them regularly. Among the things that you and your friends might look for are these:

1. *Rate:* Do you whiz through your speech so that words become garbled and difficult to understand? Do you speak so slowly and lethargically that you practically put everyone to sleep? Do you vary your rate, sometimes slowing down or pausing for emphasis?

2. *Volume:* Can you be heard? What happens if you are speaking in a huge room? Can you adjust? Do you ever overproject and seem to be "preaching" to the audience? Do you vary your volume, speaking either more loudly and forcefully or very softly to stress key points?

3. *Pitch:* Is your pitch pleasant to listen to? Are you ever too high pitched and squeaky? Or do you speak so quietly and with so little variation in pitch and tone that you speak in a monotone? Is your pitch mid-range and varied appropriately for emphasis and effect?

4. *Pronunciation/Articulation:* Do you pronounce all of the words in your speech correctly? Is your articulation clear and distinct or do you slur together words and phrases? Do you change "ing," to "in'," or substitute a short "i" sound for a short "e" (as when "get" becomes "git")? Do you have a discernible accent? If so, is it distracting? Do you throw in verbal fillers, like "you know," or use vocalized pauses ("um," or "uh") as fillers?

5. *Expressiveness:* Do you sound like you mean what you are saying? Do you emphasize the right words in sentences and the right key sentences in paragraphs? Do you sound sincere? If you tell the audience that they should act, do you sound like you are prepared to lead the way?

Many of the vocal characteristics just described are well within your control. You can learn to vary your rate and volume with a little concentration. Certainly you can improve your pronunciation and articulation. If, however, you have a difficulty with pitch that seems to persist despite your efforts, your southern accent endures, or your voice seems flat and expressionless, you may need to visit your college speech clinic or voice training center and work with specialists who are trained to help people improve their vocal quality.

Vocal quality is something on which speakers continuously work. Your voice will be different in the morning than in the evening. If you have been talking a lot, your voice may sound strained or harsh. As you grow older your voice will change. Certainly, striving for good breath support is important. Even so, achieving good vocal quality is a lifelong task.

Be Flexible

No matter how carefully you plan and practice in advance, some speaking situations will surprise you. You will find larger (or smaller) audiences than you expected, podiums missing, poor acoustics, or previously unannounced time constraints. If you are speaking from an outline, you will find it much easier to adapt to the particular situation in which you find yourself. Suppose you expected to find an audience of 30 traditionally clad businessmen and you found in their place a group of five or six men and women wearing jeans. Instead of standing behind a podium and speaking formally, you might want to consider sitting on a table and "chatting" with them to enhance the informality of the situation.

The foundation of flexibility is *spontaneity* and *open-mindedness*—a willingness to recognize that there are many different ways of giving a good speech and an ability to discover a "better" way whenever a situation seems to demand it. Contrary to the popular stereotype, it is not always appropriate for public speakers to stand, they do not always have to use podiums, and they can engage the audience in a dialogue, if those practices seem fitting and desirable. While some of these practices deviate from public speaking norms, they can work very well.

Sometimes adapting to the pecularities of a particular speaking situation may involve some risk. After all, if you've planned to do it one way and the situation you're in seems to suggest something different, you may feel some fear that your attempt at spontaneity will fail. Yet, every public speaking venture is accompanied by some risk. Determining what is appropriate always calls for judgment. As your experience as a public speechmaker increases, you will feel greater confidence in exercising your judgment and acting accordingly. However, regardless of the risk, adapting your speech to the conditions under which you are speaking is almost always the best route.

DEVELOPING GOOD ORAL STYLE

Speeches are not the same as essays. *The kind of language that is virtually perfect for the reader may be very difficult for the listener to comprehend. When you compose for the ear you have to take into account certain realities of the listening situation.* The listener has only one chance to understand what you are saying. She cannot pause and reread or take a break if she is tired. If you happen to use a word that she does not understand, she is stuck. She can't take the time to run and look it up in a dictionary. If you use very long or complicated sentences, she has to work through your verbal quagmire since she can't ask you to go back or to slow down. Basically, she is at your mercy.

Clearly, there are many differences between the speaking/listening and the writing/reading situation. As speakers we must be sensitive to those differences and do all we can to make ourselves readily understood. Above all, good oral style should be *clear.* And it cannot simply be clear in the long run or after moments of speculation or after several trips to the dictionary. Rather, it must be instantly intelligible.

Although there are many similarities between good written prose and effective oral language, there are also some important differences. As a speaker, for example, you will *use more personal pronouns* than you might as a writer. You use pronouns like "we, ours, I, you, and us" to adapt to the audience, to make your remarks specifically directed toward them, and to involve them in your arguments. Because of the need for clarity you will tend to use *simpler sentences (subject-verb-predicate) and shorter sentences* than you would as a writer. Of course, *some variety is important,* but I am referring to general qualities rather than absolute rules. As a speaker you are also likely to use quite a few *rhetorical questions,* to challenge the audience to think and to involve them in your presentation. You may also want to *repeat key words, phrases, and sentences* to help the audience remember them. This practice is especially useful with complicated speeches or with speeches built around a memorable theme or slogan. Finally, as a speaker you will tend to use *more contractions* than you would as a writer. Usually, writing is a more formal mode of communication than is speaking. As a speaker you want to emphasize the conversational quality of the speech. In daily conversation we rarely say, "I cannot go" or "He will not stay." Instead, we say, "I can't" and "He won't." As speakers we sound more natural when we use contractions.

As you strive to develop good oral style, you will be working largely with word choice and sentence structure. Following are some guidelines you may find useful.

1. *Whenever possible, use concrete words.* These words point to real objects and real events that the audience can associate with objective experience. As your words become more and more concrete, the pictures you paint in the minds of your audience become clearer and clearer. In contrast to abstract words, concrete words appeal to the senses. They point to something the listener can hear, touch, smell, see, or taste: pickles, chocolate, fire alarm, velvet, scrub brush, burning autumn leaves. Al-

though there are times in your speechmaking when you cannot avoid using abstract words, like love, friendship, democracy, or fear, you can clarify them by providing specific concrete illustrations and examples.

2. *You should also strive for simplicity.* Normally, simplicity and clarity are closely associated. By using simple words, you avoid being pretentious or vague. Why say "facilitate," if you can say "assist" or "help"? Simpler words are easier to say and easier to understand. They are also more characteristic of daily conversation than are their polysyllabic counterparts. Whenever you are about to use a long or obscure word, ask yourself, "Is there a simpler say to say it?"

3. *Avoid cliches and empty words.* Cliches are trite, overused expressions. Once they were probably fresh and interesting. Now, however, because of overuse, they are tired and lifeless. Among the cliches to be avoided are:

after all is said and done	last but not least
easier said than done	all in all
ignorance is bliss	reigns supreme
it goes without saying	in the final analysis
few and far between	clear as crystal
more than meets the eye	busy as a bee
light as a feather	tired but happy

Also to be avoided are empty words, which add no meaning to your sentences but only add length. Here are some empty phrases along with their more concise translations:

a majority of (most)	is designed to be (is)
a number of (many; several)	for a period of (for)
as a result of (so)	it will be necessary to (I must)
at the same time as (while)	on account of (because)
bring to a conclusion (conclude)	prior to (before)
due to the fact that (because)	with the aid of (with)
in close proximity to (near)	subsequent to (after)
in connection with (about)	in the course of (during)
in terms of (in; for)	for this reason (because)

4. *Choose precise words.* Mark Twain once observed that there is no such thing as a synonym; he admonished writers to find the right word, not its "second cousin." This is an issue that is equally applicable to speakers. Precise words are essential because they allow us to communicate accurately our meaning. If you wanted to describe someone walking down the street, how would you do it? Specifically, what verb would you

use? The correct verb to use depends entirely upon the kind of image you want to create in the minds of your listeners. Is the person in a hurry? If so, you might want to use a verb like "raced" or "hustled" or "flew." Yet, each of these is different. Which is faster? Which is more casual? Suppose you wanted to describe the way you felt toward something—in this case a negative feeling. You might say you "disliked" it, but if you felt more strongly you might use verbs like "hated," "detested," or "loathed." Which is most potent? Look them up in a dictionary. In the long run you will be more efficient and economical in your word choice. Why say "walked slowly" if you can say "ambled," or "loved very much" if you can say "adored"? Thus, precise language is usually both clear and compact.

Beside dealing with words, you also need to examine your sentences. Here are some guidelines for constructing good oral sentences.

1. *Keep the subject and the verb reasonably close together.* This practice increases the intelligibility of your sentences. Consider this sentence: "This grading system, which has been adopted by many colleges and universities around the nation and has worked very well, is worthy of your support." A much clearer way to state these ideas is as follows: "This grading system is worthy of your support. Many other colleges and universities have already adopted it with impressive results."

2. *Keep your sentences relatively short.* Although you will want some variety in sentence length and type, in general you should use relatively short sentences because they are easy for audience members to follow and understand. Avoid adding length to your sentences by using empty words, unnecessary modifiers, and needless repetition. Also eliminate circumlocutions like "*The reason why* I think this is a good idea is *because.....*" Instead, say simply "I think this is a good idea because. . . ."

3. *Whenever possible, use the active voice.* One of the best ways to delete unnecessary words is to consistently use the active voice. Compare the following:

> "Much dissatisfaction with the new graduation requirements has been expressed by the students." (passive voice)

> "Students have expressed much dissatisfaction with the new graduation requirements." (active voice)

Passive sentences are always longer than active ones. They are often unclear as well. Consider this sentence, for example: "This date was chosen for the dance because it didn't conflict with any other campus-wide events." It does not tell us who did the choosing, and if we wanted to protest the date, that could be important information.

4. *Use only necessary modifiers.* There are two kinds of modifiers in our language, those that comment and those that define. Commenting modifiers include "very," "most," and "definitely." These modifiers tell

us nothing new; rather, they try to boost the meaning of the word with which they are associated. If you choose your words with a concern for precision, you should almost never have to use a commenting modifier. However, some modifiers, like "costly," "innovative," "stubborn," or "hot," are essential; they tell us something we need to know. Defining modifiers provide information that the noun standing alone cannot convey.

5. *Strive for straightforward sentences.* Avoid beginning your sentences with an accumulation of clauses. Don't say, for instance, "When you think of the advantages of this plan, when you consider its low cost, and when you focus on its forward-looking nature, you should be convinced that we need to move forward and adopt it." A better, more straightforward way of saying this would be: "I am convinced that the plan I've outlined here tonight is the one to pursue. It is practical, inexpensive, and forward-looking." As with simple, short sentences, straightforward ones are easy for the audience to follow.

USING AUDIO-VISUAL AIDS

Suppose you were making a speech about the plight of higher education and you needed to discuss declining college enrollments at your own school and across the nation. Not only would you need to gather appropriate statistics, but, because those statistics were so central to your argument, you would need some way to highlight them, making them clear and memorable. To do this, you would probably use a visual aid—in this case, a line graph depicting the rise and fall in enrollment over a period of time.

Many speeches can be enhanced by using audio-visual aids, which add color, interest, and clarity to a presentation if they are constructed and used properly. They allow you to *show* the audience precisely what you are talking about, thus increasing the chances that you and your audience will have a common understanding.

Types of Audio-Visual Aids

1. *Objects.* Often you will make a speech that involves the discussion of some object. If that object is large enough to be seen but small enough to carry with you, you may want to bring it along to assist your presentation. You might consider, for example, bringing such things as an antique vase, your clarinet, or the works of your favorite artist. If the object you have in mind is too small, such as rare coins you have collected, you will have to resort to passing them around after your presentation. Also, think carefully before deciding to bring a pet as a visual aid. Live visuals have been known to exhibit stubbornness, make unsolicited "contributions" to the presentation, and in other ways steal the show!

2. *Models.* If, for whatever reason, the object you are discussing cannot be presented, you might want to consider using a model. One kind is a small-scale model of a large object. If, for example, you were discuss-

ing a proposed new school building, you might construct a three-dimensional model to help the audience envision the layout of the new facility. Or you might need a large-scale representation of a small object. One speaker, for instance, wanted to discuss how a watch actually works. To do this he brought a large-scale model showing the interior mechanisms of a Swiss-movement watch. Also, models can be life-size. If you wanted to teach the audience how to use cardio-pulmonary resuscitation techniques, for example, you might borrow a life-size dummy from the YMCA or the Red Cross to use in a demonstration.

3. *Chalkboard.* Since nearly every classroom is equipped with a chalkboard, most student speakers use it as a convenient means of communicating information. The chalkboard might be a sensible choice of visual support if your handwriting is legible, if you are working on a clean board, and if you can practice so that you do not lose contact with the audience while you write. Using several different chalk colors, too, can enhance the rather ordinary appearance of most chalkboards. If possible, prepare the board in advance and cover it with a curtain, to be lifted at the appropriate moment.

4. *Drawings.* Often in preparing a speech you discover that you would like to use photographs. Unless you have access to oversized enlargements, however, photographs cannot be used, except to be passed around at the end of the speech. That's why drawings, sketches, diagrams, and maps are such good alternatives. Not only are they inexpensive to make, but, since they are constructed precisely for your speech, they include only that information you want conveyed. You don't have to be an artist to create a simple, accurate drawing. Careful preparation and the skillful use of color and simplicity are all that is required. Figures 9.1 and 9.2 present sample drawings used by student speakers.

5. *Graphs.* If you are making a speech that involves the presentation of statistics, you may find graphs a good way to simplify and clarify your figures. The most common type is the *line graph.* You may want to use a line graph if you need to show comparative relationships over a period of time. Figure 9.3 presents an example of a line graph comparing the percentage of men and women holding management positions from 1920 to 1990. The *bar graph* is also commonly used. Bar graphs are useful for depicting quantity; they are especially well suited to demonstrating comparisons. Let's say, for instance, you wanted to discuss enrollments at

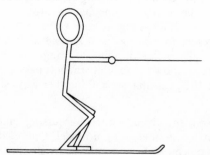

Figure 9.1 A Figure Drawing of the Appropriate Body Position for Water Skiing

Figure 9.2 A Map Depicting the Territory of the Original Thirteen States

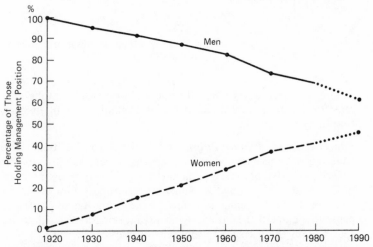

Figure 9.3 A Comparison of the Percentages of Men and Women in Management Since 1920

your college in comparison with those at another institution. Figure 9.4 depicts one form this graph might take. The *pie graph* is also commonly used. It can be used to illustrate simple distribution patterns. You will often see a pie graph in your newspaper showing the divisions of the national budget. Figure 9.5 depicts such a graph demonstrating the percentages of students at a particular college according to religious affiliations.

6. *Charts.* If you need to summarize large blocks of information, you might want to consider constructing a chart. Charts can take the form of summary tables or can be used to show relationships. Figure 9.6 depicts

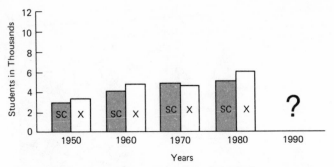

Figure 9.4   Comparing Student Body Size: State College Versus College X

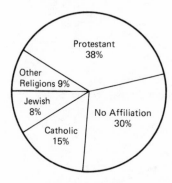

Figure 9.5   Religious Affiliation of Students at State College in 1984

a sample organization chart. In constructing either graphs or charts, refer to the guidelines listed at the end of this section. In particular, simplicity is essential.

7. *Films, Slides, and Other Projections.* Perhaps you feel that you do not have the resources available for preparing media aids for your speech. Clearly, preexisting films and filmstrips would only be used with presentations that you planned to make several times. You might want to consider, however, using an overhead projector. These use transparent pages that can either be prepared in advance or constructed during your speech with the use of a special felt-tip marker. Because the overhead projector projects the image behind you, you can write on the transparency while facing the audience, thus making it easier to use than the chalkboard. If you choose to use one of these media aids in your speech, recognize the importance of practicing. Making transitions back and forth between your speech notes and a slide projector, however, is not easy. To make it go smoothly, you need to rehearse. Of course, there is always the possibility of mechanical failure. Therefore, although media-assisted presentations can be impressive, they are accompanied by some risk.

8. *Tapes, Records, and Videos.* With some speech topics there is simply no substitute for allowing the audience to share the speaker's experiences. If these experiences have to do with *listening* to something, such as the music of John Lennon, the calls of different birds, or the humor of Benny

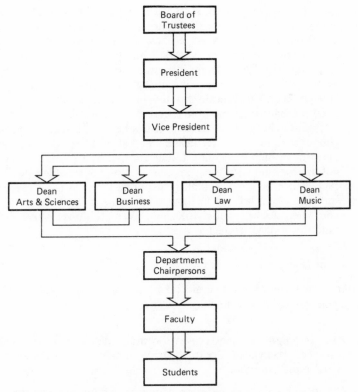

Figure 9.6 The Organization of a Typical College

Hill, you may need to bring a tape or record. Words are generally not adequate in helping listeners to feel and understand something like music. Should you decide that an audio aid is necessary for your speech, prepare it very carefully. Make sure you can quickly locate the pertinent parts of the tape or record. If necessary, prepare a tape that contains only those excerpts that you need to use for your speech. Try to arrive early and test your audio equipment to see how it sounds in the particular room in which you will be speaking; adjust the volume accordingly. Make sure that you bring the equipment you need. In the case of a videotape, make sure a video monitor is available and can accommodate your particular size and kind of videotape. As with visual aids, practice and time yourself carefully. If you have only 15 minutes, both your audio aid and your comments should last only that long.

9. *Handouts.* If you are making a speech in which you are presenting a detailed budget or have an article relevant to your speech that you would like the audience to read, you may decide to provide handouts. When preparing these visual aids, make sure you have an adequate number. Pass them out at the *end* of your presentation to make sure they do not become a source of distraction. Audience members often enjoy having something tangible to remind them of your main ideas, to present further information, or to further stimulate their interest.

10. *You.* In a sense, you are always a visual aid during every speech you make. That's why your attire, your facial expressions, and your posture are so important. In some speeches you may even choose to call attention to yourself in some way that highlights you as a focal point of visual interest. Recently, for instance, a student spoke on the ambiguity associated with nonverbal communication from one culture to the next. He demonstrated several signs and gestures that have strikingly different meanings for people from different cultures. By doing this, he called attention to himself and to the gestures he was demonstrating. Another young woman spoke on fashion and dressed so as to demonstrate different fashion principles. Using yourself as a visual aid is probably not appropriate with every speech. When you are able to do so, however, it can be good in that it encourages you to move, gesture, and sometimes to relax. It also focuses the audience's attention on you and your ideas. As with other visual aid choices, this one also requires much practice in order to feel at ease.

Guidelines for Using Audio-Visual Aids

No matter what form your visual aid takes, you will most likely have greater success if you follow these guidelines:

1. *Keep it simple.* Do not crowd too many details onto one chart; use several charts instead. Try to illustrate no more than one point with each visual representation.

2. *Clarity and color are desirable.* If you are trying to show the audience the parts of an engine, those parts as drawn on your poster board should be accurate and recognizable. If there is writing, it should be neat, clear, bold and, if appropriate, colorful. A black and white chart is not nearly as strong as one that includes red, purple, or blue. For most charts and diagrams, basic vivid colors are preferable to pastels; they are easier to decipher and can provide more contrast. Whatever color scheme you choose should enhance clarity and be pleasing to the eye.

3. *Make sure everyone can see your visual aid.* Some speakers hold up postcards and talk about their exciting trip to Europe. Only the people in the front row can see the pictures. Other speakers use an overhead projector and use such small lettering that it is impossible to read. Still others have cramped, illegible writing or show pictures from books that cannot be seen at a distance. Hence, the concept of aid turns to hinderance. Consider the needs of each audience member in presenting your aids. If necessary, walk around the room and show the visual at different angles, or hold it high so that those in the back can see. Strive for bold, legible printing or writing. Above all, make sure that you do not obscure the visual by blocking it with your own body. It is not uncommon for speakers to partially block chalkboards or charts as they discuss them.

4. *Point to the part of the aid you are discussing, but do not lose contact with the audience.* If your visual aid has more than one component, you may need to focus the audience's attention on the part being discussed by pointing to it with your finger, pencil, or some other manageable object.

However, make sure that you do not deliver your speech to the visual aid, looking only at it instead of at the audience.

5. *Display your visual aid only while you are discussing it.* If you set up a colorful chart or an intriguing model at the beginning of your speech, many audience members will begin to focus on it right away, wondering what it is and how you are going to use it. That takes attention away from you. Similarly, when you are finished discussing your visual aid, remove it from sight so that the audience returns their attention to you.

6. *Use only justified visual aids.* Many speeches do not need visual aids. If you are discussing the reasons your classmates should vote to abolish final examinations, you would have little need of a visual aid. Never use a visual aid just because it would "jazz up" your presentation. Use only those visuals that are needed for purposes of clarity, concreteness, or interest.

7. *Practice with your visual aid before the speech.* Make sure you are comfortable with the equipment if you are using an overhead or a slide projector. Practice moving back and forth from the chalkboard or posterboards without losing your train of thought. You should do all you can to smoothly integrate your visual materials into your presentation.

HANDLING AUDIENCE PARTICIPATION

Most of the time after you make a speech you will be asked to entertain questions. The question-response or *forum period* is particularly important because during this time you will have an opportunity to interact directly and informally with the audience—to provide added information, to build further your credibility, and to deal perhaps with aspects of your topic untouched by the speech itself. Some speakers give little thought to the questioning period. Instead, they focus all of their attention on the formal speech itself. Yet, many speakers have damaged their credibility while attempting to respond to audience questions. They have revealed their ignorance, defensiveness, or prejudice through thoughtless or uncaring responses. That's why it is so important to recognize that the forum period is a potentially crucial part of the public speaking event. If you handle audience questions well, you can make your message more compelling; but poor responses can result in weakening your case.

The following general guidelines may assist you in preparing for forum periods.

1. *Listen carefully to each question posed.* If you can't hear the questioner very well, ask her to stand and repeat the question. Or move away from the podium and stand closer to the audience so that you can interact more directly. As you listen, provide a few nonverbal cues, like head nods, to let the questioner know that you are attentive and are following the point she is addressing.

2. *If appropriate, repeat each question* so that everyone can hear it and keep track of what is happening. In repeating the question you may need to

rephrase it, since often audience members will phrase their questions in awkward or rambling ways.

3. *Do not allow any one person to dominate the forum period.* If many people raise their hands at once, make sure you call on ones who have not spoken previously. Or if the same person who has already posed a question raises his hand again, you might ask, "Is there anyone with a question who has not yet spoken?" Occasionally, a persistent questioner may pursue you and try to engage you in dialogue for an extended period of time. If that is the case, you might ask that person to remain afterward so that you might continue to talk privately.

4. *Don't try to fake your way through a response.* If you don't know the answer, say so. Someone may ask you, for example, if you have read a particular book that relates to your presentation. If you haven't but you say you have (so as to appear well versed), you will find yourself in an even tougher spot when the questioner next asks, "What did you think of the author's view of self-actualization?" At this point you are really in trouble! Admitting that you do not know the answer to a particular question is not the end of the world. Besides, you may be able to relate it to something you do know; for example, you might say, "I haven't read that book, but I just finished one that sounds very similar to it," and then go on to talk about it. You can also use this as an opportunity to jot down the information provided by the audience member, thus demonstrating that you too are willing to learn and grow. In this way you highlight the reality that even public speaking is a two-way communication process.

5. *Respect time limits.* Question and answer periods cannot go on forever. They, like speeches, occur within a time constraint. On some occasions you will be asked to speak briefly and leave a good deal of time for responding to questions. Other times you will make a longer speech and only have time to take two or three questions. What is important is that you ask in advance what the audience expects or desires. If you speak for most of the allocated time and do a very good job, you may yet hurt your cause if several audience members leave feeling frustrated because they were not given the chance to ask their questions or air their points of view. Similarly, if you leave lots of time for questions when the audience expected your speech to fill up the entire program time, you may leave them with the impression that you didn't prepare carefully or didn't have very much to say. Both negative outcomes can be avoided by simply asking what is expected and by following through.

6. *If appropriate, encourage audience members to participate.* On some occasions you may make the kind of speech that is bound to generate strong audience response. Or perhaps you have presented a lot of new information, and you want to find out whether audience members followed you. In these instances you may want to solicit actively audience participation. You may choose to do this by starting in a very general way with, "Are there any questions?" That approach, however, is very broad and doesn't provide any cues as to the kinds of questions or

comments that might be appropriate. Remember that many audience members experience their own form of speech anxiety; that is, they are reluctant to speak up in front of their peers in the audience. Thus, you may have to encourage them. One way to do this is to ask a more specific question, like, "How do you react to the idea of forced busing?" That signals an area of potential controversy and says, in effect, "This would be a good area for us to pursue." In this way audience members will recognize that you see this subject as one worthy of some dialogue. If you know that a specific person in the audience has had experience with your subject, you might turn to her and pose a question. For example, if you were discussing how to be an effective manager and you knew that someone in your audience had had ten years of management experience, you might ask, "How does this management theory relate to your experiences as a manager, Eileen?" Of course, you must be very careful as you target audience members that you do not embarrass them. Only ask questions of those who clearly are listening, and make sure your questions do not request information that the individual is unlikely to have. Finally, one good way to encourage the audience to talk with you is to move from behind the podium, lean against something, or even sit down on a table or desk, reinforcing the notion of informal exchange and removing potential status barriers between you and your audience.

IN CONCLUSION

Many teachers of public speaking talk with their students about content, organization, and delivery as if they were distinct categories of speaking skills. This, however, is hardly the case. They are completely interdependent. You need to be effective in all of these areas if you want to excel as a public speaker. What you say, the language you use to express it, the way you arrange your ideas, and the manner in which you present yourself and your ideas are equally crucial. Even if you choose a good topic, narrow it and focus it appropriately, engage in extensive research, and work to select the most fitting pattern of organization, you need also to make the final commitment of time and energy to present your ideas in interesting, colorful language and to practice your delivery so that you are articulate and compelling.

Learning to be a good public speaker involves a process of growth. As you grow as a public communicator, you will make mistakes. You will encounter frustration, confusion, and sometimes feelings of failure. But if you follow the principles recommended in this book, and if you are willing to work very hard, you will improve. Most people are not born with exceptional public speaking talent. They develop it by reading great speeches, listening to good speakers, reading books about public speaking, and practicing for hours and hours. You may give several speeches or even several dozen speeches before you feel that you are really good at speaking in public. Or you may never be entirely satisfied with your performance. What is important, however, is that you continue to work at it, study your mistakes, seek feedback from others, and try once again. No growth process is easy. However, if you want to become an excellent public speaker the chances are very good that, with commitment and time, you will accomplish your objective.

EXERCISES

1. Watch for announcements of public speakers who are going to be on your campus or in your community. Choose one whose topic is of interest to you. Attend the speech. For this speaking event, plan to focus on the speaker's delivery and language. In particular, note the following:

> Gestures/movement
> Eye contact
> Vocal quality (rate, pitch, expressiveness)
> Use of notes
> Use of visual aids
> Handling of audience questions
> Oral style (concreteness, simplicity, precision, etc.)

For each of these categories take notes on the speaker's communication behavior. Then assume that the speaker has asked you for your feedback. Develop a list of his or her strengths and weaknesses with at least two suggestions for improvement.

2. After carefully preparing a speech on a topic of your choice, practice talking through it aloud. If possible, speak into a tape recorder, play it back, and listen to the way you sound. How do you react to your own voice? To what extent is your voice expressive? What about your fluency? Are you too fast or slow? Too loud or soft? Now practice the speech again. This time stand before a mirror and observe your gestures, facial expressions, eye contact, etc. How might you improve these aspects of your delivery? Now relax and without either watching or taping yourself, practice your speech three or four more times. Be sure to take some breaks between practice sessions.

When you feel ready to have a "final" practice, deliver your speech one last time in front of your mirror while tape recording yourself. Observe the changes/improvements in your delivery. Note any added changes you want to make before delivering your speech to an appropriate audience.

3. Go to the library and find a book of speeches. One excellent source is *Contemporary American Speeches* by Linkugel, Allen, and Johanneson (published by Wadsworth Publishing Col, Inc., Belmont, Calif., third edition, 1972). Choose a speech written by a speaker known for his or her language skills, e.g., John F. Kennedy, Abraham Lincoln, William Jennings Bryan, or Adlai Stevenson. Read the speech carefully. Then do the following: From the speech, make a list of at least ten words that are especially concrete. In terms of precision examine the verbs used. List a half dozen of those that rate highly. Find at least five examples of simple words or phrases. Note the approximate length of the typical sentence. To what extent is the language colorful and interesting? Report your findings to your class.

4. Deliver a speech to a group. Ask them to comment on your delivery. In particular, ask them to focus on three or four aspects of delivery or language with which you have been working for some time.

After your speech is finished, ask for their reactions. Ask them to be as specific as possible. Encourage them to make concrete suggestions for improvements.

Listen to several speeches by your peers. Provide feedback. Then break into five groups. Each group should represent a speech improvement area—i.e., a group on eye contact, using visual aids, delivery style, gestures, and vocal quality. Individuals should join a group on the basis of his or her self-perceived need for improvement in the area.

For at least fifteen minutes sit in groups and brainstorm concerning strategies for improvement in the focal area. Make a note of those that seem helpful to you.

During your next round of speeches, ask the members of your group to comment on the extent to which you were able successfully to implement some of their suggestions.

Appendix

As you read each of the speeches appearing in Appendix, please react to each of the following questions. Be as specific as possible.

1. What kind of attention-getting device did the speaker use?
2. Was it effective? Why or why not?
3. Did the speaker orient the audience? How? Preview? Purpose statement? Providing historical background? Defining terms? Other?
4. What was the speaker's *purpose?* Was it clear? Was it related to some desired audience response?
5. In general, were the speaker's ideas clearly related to his or her purpose?
6. What pattern of organization did the speaker use?
7. Given the speaker's purpose, did this pattern seem appropriate? Would another pattern have been more appropriate? If so, what?
8. Did the speaker use good transitions in moving from point to point? Give at least two examples (either positive or negative).
9. What kinds of evidence did the speaker use?
10. What did you think of the quality of the speaker's evidence? Discuss at least three examples.
11. What sorts of reasoning processes did the speaker use?
12. Could you detect any reasoning fallacies? If so, what were they?
13. What did you think of the speaker's language? Clear? Precise? Simple?
14. Did the speaker make any attempt to involve the listeners in his/her speech? How?
15. Did the speaker seem credible as a source of information on this topic? Why or why not?

The Future Is Now*

A ZEST FOR LIVING

By Walter F. Stromer, Professor, Department of Theatre and Speech, Cornell College

Delivered at a Preschool Conference at the Indiana School for the Blind, Indianapolis, Indiana, April 23, 1982

When a man has to travel four hundred miles to find an audience to listen to him you have to wonder how things are going for him back home. But my excuse for being here is that some wonderful people who heard me speak years ago have been kind enough to invite me back and that kind of flattery is hard to resist.

When I was told that the title of this talk was to be "The Future Is Now," I was puzzled. When I was also told that it had been suggested by a psychiatrist, my first impulse was to turn the tables and to analyze the analyst. On second thought, I decided that this was a topic I could live with and that it expresses something which I truly believe. I feel strongly that we should learn from the past and that we have a responsibility to those who come after us, but that the most important task for us is to live this day and this moment to the best of our ability.

Since many of you here are parents of blind children, I want to talk first about what has been done in the past for the blind and other handicapped. Then I want to make some tentative suggestions that may be of help to you in the future, which begins now.

Those wonderful Greeks of twenty-five hundred years ago, to whom we owe so much, used to put defective babies in clay jars beside the road and let them die. In Rome such children were put into wicker baskets and put out on the Tiber river, to be swept away and drowned somewhere downstream. In many countries defective babies were staked out on the mountains to die of exposure or to be eaten by animals.

These earlier ancestors of ours were not entirely lacking in compassion; but, they were often in real danger of being exterminated by famine or flood or marauding enemies, and survival of the group had to be put ahead of survival of the weakest members who could not help themselves. Caring for the handicapped, as we know it, could not really take place until societies became somewhat stable and had some surplus food and some leisure time for some members.

Lack of resources was not the only factor that kept society from humane treatment of its disabled members. Attitudes were also involved. Epilepsy was once thought to be caused by the moon. To be moonstruck was to be deranged or insane. What we call mental illness was once attributed to possession by demons, who in one case in the Bible were driven out of the man into a herd of swine. Blindness and other conditions were connected with sin, as when the disciples asked Christ, about the blind man, "Who sinned, this man or his parents?" As long as the causes of disability are thought to be supernatural, either godly or satanic, the only cure will have to be supernatural, such as prayers, incantations or exorcisms; but, not much will get done at the local human level.

---

*From Vital Speeches of the Day, vol. 16, June 1, 1982.

Slowly attitudes began to change. In the 4th Century A.D., a Christian bishop urged compassion for the retarded. In the 9th Century in Baghdad, the Caliph ordered that those getting out of hospitals should be given a sum of money to tide them over until they could go to work. Yet, at this same time, in other parts of Europe people were being blinded for committing such crimes as poaching, that is hunting on land which they did not own. Ironically the church fathers of that day approved of blinding instead of putting the person to death because they felt that blinding would give the victim more time to repent of his sins.

Centuries later the defectives—the stutterers, those with pointed heads, the grossly deformed—were exhibited in cages, in carnivals and sideshows for the amusement and amazement of the public. After that, came the asylums and the institutions where the defectives were locked away. Others were locked away in attics or back bedrooms until their tortured bodies became torturing skeletons in the family closet.

As late as World War II, the Federal government did not include blind people in this country as eligible for rehabilitation funds. It was thought that they could not be rehabilitated but would simply have to exist on welfare. Consider how far we have come. Last year was the International Year of the Disabled Person. This year has been declared the National Year of the Disabled Person in this country. We know that there are between 30 and 40 million disabled persons in this country and about 450 million in the world. Just the fact that we can count them, even approximately, is a mark of our progress. In the Middle Ages young children were not even counted in the census because it was assumed that most of them would die by the age of twelve. Why bother counting?

Another indication of our concern and our openness to the subject is the fact that there are 120 organizations for disabled. There are more than 130 wheelchair basketball teams. A totally deaf woman holds the world speed record for driving a vehicle on land. The president of Hofstra University is a man with cerebral palsy. Recently a young blind woman was involved in down-hill skiing competition in Switzerland, while two other blind skiers and four sighted companions set out to ski across Lapland.

In the area of entertainment, we have had the play *Butterflies are Free,* about a blind young man, and *Whose Life Is it, Anyway?*, about a quadraplegic veteran. The movie *Inside Moves* deals with disabilities. The television movie, *Elephant Man,* dealt with one who was grossly deformed. A retarded boy was permitted to play himself in a movie about the retarded instead of having the role played by a professional actor. From Seattle, you can rent a film about a boy who lost both legs and went on to become a football coach. In Dallas, a television station devotes several minutes each day to advertising available children. These children are not for sale for immoral purposes but they are handicapped children available for adoption.

Yet with all this progress we must admit that there are still problems. Many of them are in the area of employment. Of those who are paralyzed, almost 90 percent are unemployed. Of the blind, Job Opportunities for the Blind estimates that 70 percent of the blind are unemployed or underemployed. Harold Krents, graduate of Harvard Law School, and inspiration for the movie and play, *Butter-flies are Free,* applied to forty law firms before he got a job.

Taking it all together, the good and the bad, I think it is not unreasonable to say that if one must live as a handicapped person, this time and this place is one of the best that history has known.

Next, I would like to talk especially to those of you who are parents of blind children about some tentative suggestions as to how you can help your child and yourself. I do this with some hesitation because I knew so much more about child rearing before we had children than I do now.

One of the first things you can do is to believe sincerely that raw fish tastes good. I use this example because we have a Japanese student who has stayed with us often who assures me that raw fish is delicious. My mind says it's true. My stomach says, don't touch it. It is hard for us really to believe that people can enjoy food which we consider repulsive. In the same way, it is hard for us to believe that others can be happy without all the things that make us happy. For example, people will look at one who is blind and say, "How terrible, how tragic, how miserable it must be without sight." Yet, I can assure you from my personal experience and from contact with many blind people, that blindness need not result in constant unhappiness. Keep in mind that we have no reliable external measures of happiness, no brain scan, no blood test. About the best we can do is to ask people if they are happy. While I may be better informed on the happiness of blind people than you, still when it comes to deaf-blindness, my own reaction is very similar to yours. I find myself thinking, "How tragic, how difficult." I read recently about a man and wife, both deaf-blind, taking training at the Helen Keller Center on Long Island. When they want to communicate, one goes to the kitchen table and pounds on it to make the floor vibrate. Then they meet at the table and if they are angry they spell words into each others hands rapidly. My reaction was, "How tragic, how inadequate, how frustrating. How much better it would be if they could shout at each other, or better still if they could see each other and make faces." Or would it be better? Who are we to say that their way of communicating feelings or frustration is better or worse than ours. This same deaf-blind man laid tile for his basement floor; he hung paper on the walls of his kitchen, and he travels around the city by subway. Is he less happy than we are? I doubt it. Yes, he does miss out on things you and I take for granted. Is he aware of what he is missing? Yes, to some extent I am sure the deaf-blind are aware that life could be simpler and less frustrating if they could see or hear, or both. But I doubt that they spend much time fretting about it. In general, it seems to be the nature of living organisms to adapt as best they can to the circumstances that exist. Does the worm wish it could fly like the robin? Does the robin regret not having the wings of an eagle? But you will say people are different from the lower animals. Yes, they are. Yes, humans can worry and envy and regret. Still, it is amazing how people with stable personalities can have their bodies broken and pick up the few remaining pieces and make a life of them.

You and I can help handicapped people by letting them define happiness for themselves. We can make life more miserable for them if we constantly remind them of how terrible we feel because of what they are missing. When we do that we are really saying to them, "Please get rid of your handicap because it makes me so uncomfortable."

Let me illustrate how disabled people can be happy in their ignorance. Sometimes during a long Iowa winter I walk to class in the morning and decide it's a nice day because I can feel the sun warming my back. Then some sighted person comes along and says, "It's such a dull, depressing day." To him it is dull because the sun is under the clouds. That doesn't really destroy my happiness, and I do need to be aware that other people perceive the world in ways other than I do. I need to recognize that, just as I need to turn on lights in a room for the benefit of others even though I don't need them. So I will continue to be happy about the warm sun while my friend is depressed by the gray clouds. And, on other days, I will be depressed by the cold while he enjoys the bright, but cold, sunshine. We can each find happiness in our own way.

Is this so different from what happens to any of you? You are all missing out on some success or happiness. You fathers are all disabled in some ways. Some of you are too short to be successful basketball players, and others of you are too scrawny to be professional football players. Do you cry yourselves to sleep every night because of what you are missing? I doubt it. And, you mothers who are lacking the face or the figure to appear on a movie screen, do you beat your fists on the kitchen counter all day and moan about the things you can't do? I'm sure you go on with the business of living and do the best you can. Allow handicapped persons to do the same. If they like raw fish, let them eat it.

My next suggestion for you as parents is that you be like the character in magazine ads for Hastings piston rings years ago. They showed a picture of a big muscle man with a scroungy beard with a friendly smile, and the caption was, "Tough, but oh so gentle." That is a good motto for parents—to be tough, but gentle. It is especially apt for the parents of handicapped children. Just being a parent, of any child, means that you have to be gentle and protective or the child will not survive the first few years of life. Yet, somewhere along the way, you have to be as tough as the mother bear who cuffs the cubs on the snout to let them know that now is the time to leave home and get out on their own. It will be especially hard for you as parents of a blind child to watch your child bump into things or get cut and bruised and still to sit back calmly and say, "live and learn." But handicapped children, more than others, need to have such toughening experiences if they are to grow up as study oaks instead of delicate African violets. All through life, society will tend to overprotect and shelter those who are disabled. They will need a little extra measure of toughness, of assertiveness, of independence if they are to get their fair share of rights and freedoms. It may help you in learning to be tough if you will remember that most of the accidents that happen to blind people are not serious, and almost never fatal. The greatest damage is always to the loved ones who watch things happen, and to the pride of the blind or disabled person.

Last winter I was hurrying to the chapel for a convocation program. I took a short cut along a narrow sidewalk, got too far off to the left side, and got clipped just above my left eye by a tree branch stump where it had been cut off. The branch drew blood, and I knew it. I had no more than sat down in the chapel than one of my students came along and said, "Oh, you're hurt; are you all right?" I said, "Yes," and I wanted to tell him to go away and let me suffer in silence. After chapel, I did not want to go back to the office because I knew the secretary would notice and make a fuss. I didn't even want to go home for lunch because I thought my wife would wrap me in bandages and keep me in the house for a month. What was hurt was my pride. I had demonstrated to others that I was careless, or worse, that blind people can't walk across the campus without bumping into things.

You can help most if you will encourage your child to be independent, to move out, to take risks. If there is a cut or a bruise, be cheerful about cleaning it up and applying a Bandaid and then go about your business. If you can do that, you will be saying most eloquently to your child, "I have confidence in you; keep trying."

My last suggestion to you is to believe in yourself. You are here at this conference to get help and reassurance from various experts. I am sure they have much to offer and I hope you will learn from them. Never forget that in one way you are more expert than any teacher, counselor or psychiatrist you will ever meet. You are expert in knowing how it feels to have your life and your life blood wrapped up in a handicapped child, and to live with that investment twenty-four hours a day, every day of the year. That is very different from being a professional helper who deals with the problem for an hour a week, or an hour a day, or even six hours a day. We need professionals who can be detached and objective and sometimes we, as parents, need to learn some of that detachment of perspective. If ever the professional helpers get so detached that they forget the depth of your feelings, please feel free to remind them that you, too, have some expertise. Some years ago, I came across a book by a French psychoanalyst, Alfred Adler. In the first chapter of his book he wrote, "When parents come to me with a problem about their child and they tell me what they have been doing, my first response is to say, "I think you're on the right track," because parents carry a heavy burden and they need all the support they can get." I wish I could meet that psychoanalyst and hug him and say, "Thank you for understanding."

I want you to learn all you can from the professionals here or wherever you are. I might even agree with them that you need to change your behavior in some ways. I do not want you to feel that you are stupid and worthless and that you are not doing anything right. If you do that, you won't be a good role model for your child. I want your child to be happy, but part of that will come about if your child sees you as parents who find life enjoyable and challenging. So—listen to the experts, but also trust yourself.

If I may summarize briefly, let me remind you how far we have come in a mere two thousand years, such a little time in the long history of the world. Next, believe in raw fish; that is, give handicapped people much freedom in deciding what they enjoy. Try to be both tough and gentle; and, finally, listen to others but also trust yourself. I think the greatest gift you can give your child is a zest for living, a spirit of wonder and adventure, and a confidence that the problems of life can be solved or endured.

In the words of a Chancellor who was both a tyrant and a romantic, Otto von Bismarck, "With confidence in God, put on the spurs and let the wild horse of life fly with you over stones and hedges, prepared to break your neck, but always, always, without fear."

If that is a bit too romantic, let me suggest two lines from a Kipling poem. A Russian who spent seven years in Siberia said that these lines helped sustain him. And, if you will update the sexist language to make it "man or woman," perhaps these lines will help you begin the future now: "If you can fill the unforgiving minute with sixty seconds worth of distance run, yours is the world and all that's in it, and which is more, you'll be a man, my son."

The Age of Gerontion*

Diane Klemme

This speech by Diane Klemme won first place in the Women's Division of the Ninety-Seventh Annual Contest sponsored by the Interstate Oratorical Association. The event was held in West Yellowstone, Montana, May, 1970. Miss Klemme represented the state of Michigan; she is from Wayne State University.

1   She turned seventy-five last December. A year ago her husband suffered a cerebral hemorrhage which crippled and killed him before my grandmother's shocked eyes. Now she lives alone in the house she shared with grandfather for half a century, economically independent, proud that she can provide for herself in these her later years. Yet her independence cannot compensate for the limited mobility which isolates her from family and friends. Her pride cannot quell the fear she experiences daily: fear of assault and robbery by someone tempted by her slow steps and faltering cane.

2   Perhaps the problems of the independent elderly could be eased if they resided in a rest home or in the home of a relative. But in a home the aging often exchange problems of fear and isolation for problems of dehumanization and dependency. The twenty-three thousand rest homes in America servicing patients between the ages of sixty and eighty years for a period of five to ten years reduce the aging from human beings to statistics. Moreover in the home of a relative the aging member frequently assumes the position of a dependent child: a sixty-four-year-old mother who has enjoyed the domain of her own kitchen for forty years is pushed from the pots and simmering casseroles by an everwatchful, overzealous daughter determined to have her mother "relax" after years of housework; a fifty-seven-year-old widower so accustomed to juggling finances to educate three sons at college is not consulted when financial questions arise. Although the aging American may choose residency which guarantees economic well-being, he all too often sacrifices human dignity.

3   Either independent but fearful and immobile, or secure physically and socially but reduced to dependency—these are the circumstances in which the aging and aged find themselves, a limbo described byt T. S. Eliot in "Gerontion":

> Here I am, an old man in a dry month,
> Being read to by a boy, waiting for rain . . .
> I have lost my sight, smell, hearing, taste and touch,
> How should I use them for your closer contact?

4   Closer human contact between the aging American and succeeding generations has been prevented by a cycle of perceptions which defines a role for the elderly. Although the perceptions interact, the cycle can be sifted, and each perception analyzed: first, societal perception of the aging; second, familial perception; finally, the perception of the aging individual himself.

5   How do we as a society perceive the aging? In a culture that measures

*Reprinted from *Contemporary American Speeches*.

a man's worth on the basis of his productivity, those who age, who deteriorate physically and mentally are considered nonproductive. Sociologist Ruth Cavan indicates that ninety percent of the male heads of households find full-time employment before their sixty-fifth birthday; yet after they reach sixty-five, only thirty-four percent can hope for even part-time employment. And the "magical number" of sixty-five is being lowered. Industries like Ford Motor Company, feeling the pinch of inflation, have trimmed costs by trimming departments; those first considered for "Special Early Retirement" are fifty-five-year-olds deemed less productive than their younger colleagues. Society, therefore, perceives the aging as less productive, better suited to hobbies or to charity work.

6   Turning from the society that disclaims his usefulness, the aging American seeks understanding from his family, but even within the family, perceptions have changed; close human contact is denied. The children that he once fed, clothed, and educated, whose stories he patiently listened to at the dinnertable—these children have grown, married, and raised children of their own; the son and daughter of the widower ignored in financial decisions and the mother hustled from the kitchen no longer perceive themselves as dependent children owing allegiance to a self-sufficient parent, rather the parents have become dependent, obligations, even burdens. The daughter might explain, "Mother has her own room which Tommy had to give up; we make no demands on her. She doesn't even have to come to the dinnertable. What more can she want?" Or the son might rationalize, "Dad doesn't support himself on his own income like my wife and I do. He's no different in this case than our ten-year-old son. Why should he have any more to say about how we spend our money than our son does?" The supporting children may also attempt to alter the life style of the parent, simply to spare themselves problems of adjustment. In the book *You and Your Aging Parents,* Doctors Stern and Ross report a case in which a daughter discarded her father's old golden oak desk; for her the desk was an eyesore which she quickly removed, but to her father the desk had been a catch-all of memories, a place where he had studied late into the night to gain a degree and a better position, a place where his children had run for help with their homework.

7   Ostracized from society and deposed from independence by families— these are the circumstances of aging Americans. It is not surprising, then, that they perceive the role designed for them as less than a full life, an existence within the confines of the decisions of others. But the elderly only gradually assume that role. A man's children leave his house to begin families of their own; he retires and putters about the garden. The neighborhood shifts and changes around him; he no longer knows the names of his neighbors across the street; he only knows that their rowdy children trample the lawn he trims with ever-increasing difficulty. He finds himself reading the obituary columns of the newspaper to learn of the deaths of friends, former employers. One day the woman with whom he has spent a lifetime dies; to him her death is a betrayal, for by her death he becomes completely isolated from human contact. And so he lives in memories, but these too are stripped from him as easily as a daughter removes an old golden

oak desk. Finally he becomes like the widow in *Dandelion Wine,* convinced by the neighborhood children that she has never been young:

> "How old are you, Mrs. Bentley?"
> "Seventy-two."
> "How old were you fifty years ago?"
> "Seventy-two."
> "You weren't ever young?"
> "Never."
> "Never in a million trillion years?"
> "Never in a million trillion years."

8 The cycle is complete: perceptions of society, family, and individual carve an existence for the aging. And underlying the cycle there roots rejection of age, fear of dying. Our culture denies age by emphasizing youth. The media claims that to be over thirty is to be old. "The Jackie Gleason Show" will be cancelled because it appeals to viewers who purchase less than their younger counterparts. A NASA scientist observed that a younger man's PHD commands more options on the academic market. The tempo and fashions of our culture further the myth. Soft drinks like Pepsi are "for those who think young." Hair stylists tout coiffures which conceal balding spots of sensitive customers. *Bazaar* magazine runs an ad displaying a bare midriff as the female face of the future—a face both young and beautiful. We celebrate Aquarius.

9 We celebrate youth because we fear dying. As historian Arnold Toynbee explains:

> Death is un-American. If the fact of death were once admitted to be a reality even in the United States, then it would also have to be admitted that the United States is not [an] earthly paradise.

Denial of age and fear of death underlie the cycle which dictates the role of the aging. The Age of Aquarius refuses to acknowledge the Age of Gerontion.

10 How can the cycle be broken so that the aging may fulfill dignifying roles? First, realize that the decades past fifty constitute a significant portion of human existence. Recently, an ad in *Newsweek* magazine announced: "If you were born in 1919, then you shouldn't be reading this ad. You're supposed to be dead." Life expectancy is no longer fifty years, but more than seventy years: a man remains dependent for twenty years, becomes independent for thirty-five years, then lives another twenty years in retirement—almost one-third of his life.

11 In that latter third of life, the aging must realize that as past options end, new options arise for creating an existence which does not merely "use up" the years remaining. Rather than allowing others to define the Age of Gerontion for what it is not, the aging themselves can redefine later life for what it is and can be. It is a season for intellectual betterment dictated not by professional demands but by personal goals as a sixty-seven-year-old student at Oakland University demonstrates; having sold his pickle factory to the Vlasic Company, Mr. Schucart seeks a bachelor's degree in philosophy, attending every term except the winter semester. Aging is also a season for assisting a family with advice and counsel without the burden of maintaining that family. It is a season for preservation of life styles not simply materialistic as the father of a young professor at my university has discovered; a restauranteur for four decades, he has an old world finesse which enhances the atmosphere of the modern restaurant in which he serves. Younger men may serve fifteen tables while he caters to ten, yet who would judge his charming but slower style less productive?

12   But those of us who have yet to age and those who approach the reflective season of our lives must also begin now to alter the cycle, to ensure options for ourselves as we grow older. With political action we can ensure that rest homes are made less impersonal by skilled, compassionate employees, we can enact legislation making it profitable for industry to use merit, not age, as criterion for retirement. With community resources, we can provide the aging options for travel; one Michigan Community offered reduced rates to senior citizens touring Europe last year. Individually, we must acknowledge that each of us will see the dry month; we must take time now to plan activities, to provide our own options for the latter third of our lives.

13   In a society which seeks to perpetuate longevity, we can no longer afford to celebrate youth and deny age. Both young and aging alike must work to overcome the cycle which deems age unproductive and burdensome. Only then can we answer Eliot's questioning Gerontion. The answer Justice Oliver Wendell Holmes provided on his ninetieth birthday:

> The race is over, but the work never is done while the power to work remains
> . . . For to live is to function . . . And so I end with a line from [the] Latin poet:
> 'Death plucks my ear and says, Live—I am coming.'

Cancer Prevention Study II: The Right Questions for Needed Answers*

Karen Bruner Stroup, Writer
Gerda Fogle, Consultant

This speech was developed for use in the state of Indiana by a speech writer for the American Cancer Society.

Three questions that I hope you never ask in your lifetime are, "How long do I have to live?", "What are my chances for survival?", and "Why do I have cancer?". Imagine that it is you asking those questions—how would you feel? Afraid? Fearful? Helpless?

My speech today has two purposes; first, to examine our fear of cancer and second, to discuss how that fear can be overcome to aid progress in cancer research. During the second part of my speech, I'd like to focus on a very special project of the American Cancer Society, Cancer Prevention Study II, as one example of an action being taken to find out more about cancer.

Fear is a very natural human response to anything we don't understand, or to something that is unknown, that can't be seen, touched, or controlled in predictive fashion. And cancer, by its very nature, is unpredictable. Cancer is an unplanned, disorganized division of body cells. The disorganized cells invade healthy organs and create a mass of excess tissue—a tumor—which if not detected early—spreads into other parts of the body. Cancer is feared by all of us. But much of that fear comes from not understanding how to recognize causes, preventative measures, and the presence of the disease until a physician confirms our unspoken suspicions.

Fear unfortunately has a way of silencing even the most curious of minds. Few of us talk openly about cancer—believing that once confirmed, it is an automatic sentence of death—*which it is not.* Our pessimistic and fearful outlook on cancer reminds me of Mark Twain's answer when asked his opinion of Richard Wagner's music—"It's probably better than it sounds."

For the most part, cancer doesn't sound too good. The number of human lives affected by cancer in this country each year *is* staggering. Cancer strikes indiscriminately, paying little attention to social status, age, income level, and education. In Indiana alone, some 20,000 Hoosiers will battle cancer this year. And chances are that each of you here today knows someone who has been affiliated with cancer. On a national scale current figures for 1982 estimate that about 835,000 people will be diagnosed as having cancer.

Perhaps our conditioned pessimism might be altered somewhat to know that there is another side to those numbers—today, there are three million Americans ALIVE who once had cancer. Most of use are familiar with the statistic that one out of four persons will contract cancer, but remember—that also means that three out of four persons will NOT. There are people who are beating cancer—and even more than that—they are beating the fear of cancer as well. Susan almost withdrew from the world because of her cancer. But her friends weren't much help. They weren't sure how to respond to her—now that she had lost her

---

*Reprinted with permission from the authors.

hair from chemotherapy treatments, had lost weight, and worried about dying instead of dating. Her friends were fearful—and understandably so—of something they didn't understand. What it took was a rose from a 20 year old young man—given to Susan one day because he thought she was pretty—to put the spark back into her eyes. That spark has remained there—Susan continues regular chemotherapy treatments and plans to attend college this fall.

What it took was someone to look beyond the word "cancer" to see a young girl who was scared, who was letting her fears and those of others dictate her response to cancer. A rose reminded her of how special she was—how unique. Susan is only one of the many people every year who, because of progress in cancer research and because of her own victory over fear, is alive today.

But this is a picture of progress in cancer research that few of us are exposed to in our daily lives. Instead, media reports, premature revelations of cancer research, and actions taken by the government to remove suspected carcinogens from public use tend to only build on our fears of cancer. I've talked to too many people, who like me, share a common frustration in not knowing what will be the *next* cancer-causing agent. What I see happening, in a concerned effort to alert the American public of possible cancer dangers and cures, is that the government, the media, and the medical world have cried "wolf" too many times with not enough conclusive evidence or cause. Open the morning paper, listen to the radio, or watch the evening news to discover, "DES, a Cancer Causing Agent in Meat", "Pesticides Suspected of Causing Cancer Banned", "Cancer Hazard in Plastic Wrap", "Cancer Hazard in Soft-Drink Bottles", "Children's Sleepwear Treated with Cancer-Causing TRIS", "Critics Say Carcinogens Used to Decaffeinate Coffee". The list continues—saccharin, hair dye, toxic waste, air pollution, asbestos, food dye, bacon, hot dogs, spinach, drinking water, x-rays; these items are just a few of the suspected cancer-causing culprits.

We should heed well the advice of former U.S. Supreme Court Justice Louis Brandeis who cited the danger of "drawing strong conclusions with dangerously few facts". Dr. William R. Barclay, editor of the Journal of the American Medical Association has observed that "Many of the reports. . . . that have been made public have been flawed in both design and interpretation, but have been accepted by agencies that funded them, by the news media and the public". Barclay goes on to say that while ignorance of a hazard that could cause cancer CAN be dangerous, "false information can be even MORE dangerous".

What I fear is that most of us have been so over exposed to cancer warnings that they have become meaningless. How many of you pay attention anymore to the latest news on the most recent culprit that causes cancer?

Let me take a few seconds here to review what our typical response to cancer is likely to be. We either ignore it—treating the disease somewhat like a social taboo—or we take our chances, figuring that there is nothing we can do about preventing cancer anyway. Like lightning, it may strike us or it may not. We *could* put the burden of preventing cancer entirely upon our doctors. Centuries ago in China, you paid your doctor to keep you well. If you became ill or died, you stopped paying him. If too many patients became ill or died, the doctor lost his right to practice medicine, and his head was chopped off.

Well, it's time that we ourselves stopped putting our heads immediately on the chopping block as soon as we hear the word "cancer". Cancer and our fear of it can be overcome. The best medicine to put a halt to fear is FACTS—facts produced by asking the right kinds of questions about cancer. We must begin to take on some of the responsibility for understanding cancer and its causes by examining our own lives. Most of us ask questions about cancer only after its presence has been confirmed either in ourselves or in someone we love. "Why do I have cancer?" "What are my chances for survival?" "How long do I have to live?" Remember? We need to take a more active role in understanding cancer, rather than fearing it. To do that, a different set of questions need to be asked —questions like "What are the possible causes of cancer?", or "What can *I* do to reduce my risk of contracting cancer?"

We have good reason to ask these kinds of questions. A 1981 report from the U.S. Congress Office of Technology Assessment states that studies over the last two decades yielded a variety of statements that up to 90% of cancer is associated with the environment and is therefore theoretically preventable. The report recommends that relating our exposures and behaviors to cancer occurrence is a first step in cancer prevention. The report is only one of an increasing number of findings that continue to link cancer occurrence with our environment and lifestyles. Dr. John Higginson, founding director of the eleven-nation International Agency for Research on Cancer, reported recently that diet, stress, sexual and child-bearing patterns, and tobacco and alcohol consumption could well be important factors to consider when assessing cancer's causes.

The RIGHT questions for NEEDED answers on how our lifestyles and environment relate to cancer occurrence ARE being asked and asked NOW. They're in one nationwide effort by the American Cancer Society that WILL provide NEEDED answers—Cancer Prevention Study II. This ambitious research program—which is just one of the many projects conducted by the American Cancer Society—will help change our typical response to cancer from fear to increased understanding.

Some of you may recall the first Cancer Prevention Study, a research effort begun in 1959. It helped to indict cigarette smoking as a principal cause of cancer. The study is also noted for identifying a connection between obesity and certain cancers and for describing risk factors for heart disease and stroke. But since that first study, new questions about our lifestyles and the environment need to be asked. Cancer Prevention Study II, through a long-term monitoring of a large population sample, will provide needed facts not only on what risks CONTRIBUTE to cancer, but on what factors can PREVENT cancer.

Cancer Prevention Study II runs from September 1982 to September 1988. Nationwide, more than 1,000,000 Americans contacted by 80,000 American Cancer Society volunteer researchers will complete a four page questionnaire. The questionnaire touches upon such areas of concern as saccharin, hair dye, plastics, exposure to low-level radiation, occupational exposures, and the role of diet and social relationships. It's an effort to gather data to assess the role such factors play in the occurrence of cancer. There are actually two questionnaires—one for men and one for women—that were developed by a careful and pain-staking process with well-known cancer specialists and researchers. In addition, the questionnaire has undergone 13 rigorous field testings in different states.

In Indiana, some 32,000 residents will be contacted to complete the questionnaire. In _____ County, some _____ persons will be reached by a volunteer force of _____ researchers. In _____ County, our volunteers come from all walks of life. (You might want to give examples of the types of people who will be working as volunteer researchers in your county)

Since volunteers will be administering the questionnaire, the cost of the 6 year study has been significantly reduced from a projected $100,000,000 to $13,000,000 to cover computer services, clerical help, and the analysis of information.

This study is only one of the many efforts that are being made to help remove the veil of fear and mystery that shrouds our perceptions of cancer. The work of the American Cancer Society offers unlimited opportunities to help in the fight against cancer—programs conducted by our Service and Rehabilitation volunteers for cancer patients and their families, professional education seminars for health care professionals on cancer treatment and prevention, and the work of our public education and information teams touch but a few of the ways we are getting out more information to people about cancer.

Questions asked out of fear such as the ones I asked at the beginning of this speech—"How long do I have to live?", "What are my chances for survival?" and "Why do I have cancer?"—mean an unnecessary halt to the steady progress being made in our understanding of cancer; its cures, causes and prevention. If I leave you with anything from this speech, let it be these words—DON'T FEAR CANCER. It took me a long time to say those words myself, but once said and repeated and repeated, I found myself able to start asking the right questions and wanting to understand, not fear, this disease. Asking questions IS the first step to fighting cancer. Cancer is not, as Sir Winston Churchill described Russia in 1939, "a riddle wrapped inside an enigma". Start asking questions and you'll find my words to be true.

In closing I'd like to pass out some literature to you on the seven warning signs of cancer. These facts will give you some basic information to begin asking those questions that are so important in our fight against cancer.

Index